Taking Back My Mind

My Journey Out of Depression
with Psilocybin Mushrooms

Gerardo Urias

Copyright © 2020 Gerardo Urias
All rights reserved. No part of this publication may be reproduced, distributed, downloaded, decompiled, reverse engineered, stored in or introduced into any information storage and retrieval system, or transmitted in any form, or by any means, including photocopying, recording, or other electronic or mechanical methods, now known or hereafter invented, without prior written permission of the publisher, except in the case of brief quotations embodied in critical reviews, and certain other non-commercial uses permitted by copyright law. Copyright fuels creativity, encourages diverse voices, promotes free speech, and creates a vibrant culture.

ISBN: 978-1-7134-9591-8 (ebook)
ISBN: 978-1-6700-9822-1 (paperback)

First published in the United States of America, 2020.

www.takingbackmymind.com

Note: This book relates to the author's self-experimentation with psilocybin mushrooms, the drug 3,4-Methylenedioxymethamphetamine (MDMA), as well as the health practice known as the Wim Hof Method, as it relates to treating the author's depression. It is a criminal offense in the United States of America and in many other countries, punishable by imprisonment and/or fines, to manufacture, possess, or supply psilocybin mushrooms and/or MDMA, except in connection with government-sanctioned research. You should therefore understand that this book is intended to convey the author's anecdotal experiences only. It is not intended to encourage you to break the law, and no attempt should be made to use these substances for any purpose except in a legally sanctioned clinical trial. Notwithstanding the legality or illegality of the treatment in question, no attempt at self-diagnosis or self-treatment for serious or long-term mental or physical problems should be made without first consulting a qualified medical practitioner.

Furthermore, the author is not a doctor, physician, or health care practitioner, and so the information in this book is in no way meant as medical advice and should be used for informational purposes only. This book presents a wide range of opinions about a variety of topics related to health and well-being, including certain ideas and practices that may be hazardous if undertaken without proper medical supervision. These opinions reflect the research and ideas of the author but are not intended to substitute for the services of a trained health care practitioner. Consult with your health care practitioner before engaging in any diet, drug, supplement, exercise regimen, or any other topic in this book.

The author and the publisher expressly disclaim any liability, loss, or risk, personal or otherwise, that is incurred as a consequence, directly or indirectly, of the contents of this book.

Some names have been changed for privacy.

In Loving Memory of my father, Leopoldo Urias
November 15, 1927 - April 20, 2017

For all the knowledge, strength, fortitude, resilience, courage, and love he embodied and carried forward from generations of indigenous wisdom and passed on to me.
Gracias, Papi, la lucha indígena sigue fuerte.

SUPPORT MENTAL HEALTH

All author royalties used to fund Gerardo's projects, including an upcoming documentary about Gerardo's journey, several psychedelic healing retreats in California and Mexico, more books about mental health, and psychedelic research.

CONTENTS

PRAISE FOR TAKING BACK MY MIND	6
PROLOGUE	7
IT WAS ALL A DREAM	12
DEPRESSION	17
LIBERATION	22
THE CASE FOR PSYCHEDELICS	27
ADDICTION	44
THE WIM HOF METHOD	50
YOGA & MEDITATION	60
STOIC PHILOSOPHY	68
EL HOMBRE FELIZ	83
THE VISION	94
ADDENDA	107
BULLETPROOF ROUTINE	107
CASE STUDIES	115
RESOURCES	136
ACKNOWLEDGEMENTS	143
ABOUT THE AUTHOR	147
ENDNOTES	148

PRAISE FOR TAKING BACK MY MIND

"I am reading this and crying—this is so powerful!! Thank you so much for pouring your heart into this book! OMG! I can't stop reading! This book is phenomenal! It is so emotional, it gets you down to the core and at the same time is full of evidence-based information and very deep research. You will change so many lives! Thank you for sharing your book with me; it is definitely changing my course of action!"

~ Anonymous

"This book has really changed my thought process and made me want to change my life. The author's descriptions and use of words brought my wife to tears. As someone who has struggled with depression in the past, I believe it will help a lot of people with depression. Thank you so much for writing this book!"

~ John D' Rozario

PROLOGUE

Everything you see happening is the consequence of that which you are.
~ David R. Hawkins

I experienced my first rave, Narnia, in 1997 in Snow Valley, California, where I had learned to ski when I was younger. As I watched revelers dance the chilly night away under a bright, starlit mountain sky, an enveloping wave of euphoria flooded my entire body and love permeated everything. My friends and I had taken ecstasy, the party name for MDMA, for the first time. I had never felt such bliss. Strangers instantly bonded as a deep understanding filled the air. We hugged as a group and welcomed this transformative, enlightening, and life-changing new sensation.

As our initial jitters and excitement subsided, my best friend of many years and I, inspired by the mountain setting, started entertaining the magical idea of snowboarding for an entire winter. Another friend had worked in the German Alps the year before, and I wondered if we could do something similar. Our conversation kept circling back to this seductive vision, and by the end of the night, we'd decided to contact my friend, do some research, and move to Germany for the winter. I'd never considered doing anything so crazy, but on this night, it seemed very possible. We couldn't find a flaw in the plan.

Over the next few months, we saved the little money we made and booked a one-way flight to Germany. I arrived with only $200 in my pocket, and we found work with the US Armed Forces Recreation Center at the Hausberg Ski Lodge within a few days. This crazy idea, hatched as a rave illuminated the beautiful mountain forest around us, turned into three of the most magical years I would ever experience, defining who I would become as a young adult. For this, I had MDMA to thank. It broke apart my mental blocks, dissolved any doubt, and infused my friend and me with passion. MDMA made me see that anything is possible, a truth I've never forgotten.

Arriving in Garmisch-Partenkirchen in the winter of 1997 was like stepping into a snow globe and disconnecting from the rest of the world—like living in a postcard. Garmisch-Partenkirchen, home of the 1936 Winter Olympics games, is nestled into a stunning valley on the southern border with Austria, surrounded by towering snow-capped peaks with a crystal-clear river splitting the town in half. Beautiful streams flow between city streets and under walking bridges, meandering through quaint neighborhoods. Horse carriages trot through the city as tourists take in festivals, markets, local celebrations, and delicious cuisine. We lived every day to the fullest, getting lost in the beauty of nature, the majesty of ancient castle ruins, and the rhythm of the mountains as we found ourselves. Adventure molded our young personalities as we created strong, lifelong bonds with friends along the way. It was perfect.

Shortly after we settled into our new home, we began traveling to neighboring cities and countries. We immediately fell in love with the beauty, history, and liberal culture of Amsterdam, where psilocybin mushrooms were legal. (Psychedelic mushrooms were banned in the Netherlands in 2008 after a few reckless accidents brought negative attention to them.) We began experimenting with these mushrooms, leading to some of the most magical, mystical, and transformational experiences I've ever had: peering through history in Amsterdam's canals; skiing fresh powder on the Zugspitze, Germany's highest mountain, on a clear, bluebird powder day; lying in perfect green meadows surrounded by the

Alps; swimming in pristine alpine lakes; and exploring ancient castle ruins. I was young then, and a risk taker, but I made it out alive and wouldn't change a thing. I approach psychedelics differently today, but those years set the bar for how to live. They made me fall in love with life.

For the next twenty years, I never settled. I never accepted a paycheck as the purpose of life. While the rest of my friends climbed corporate ladders, I never stopped reaching for the dream. Only once did I fall for the corporate gimmick, when I was in my early thirties, shortly before I got married. After toiling away through twelve-hour work days for a few years, I found Tim Ferris's book *The Four-Hour Workweek* while I was strolling through a Barnes & Noble. The book inspired me to move to Panama with my new wife, determined to design a lifestyle that balanced work and play.

My time in Bavaria taught me to place the highest value on experiences and spending time in nature. Money has never motivated me. I attribute that to my early experiences with MDMA and magic mushrooms—and research proving that powerful perspective shifts experienced during psychedelic journeys can have lasting effects for months, even years, backs me up.

I started researching the use of psychedelics to treat depression and anxiety after I got married in 2013 because my wife suffered from lifelong depression and anxiety. By then, it had been more than eighteen years since I had eaten psilocybin mushrooms, but I remembered the feeling fondly. Four years later, after our divorce and my father's death sent me into a debilitating depression of my own, I would find they were exactly the healing I needed.

On December 22, 2017, psilocybin liberated me from the torture of my mind. My mission ever since has been to raise awareness about these life-saving plant medicines. I suffered immensely for ten months and fell victim to pharmaceutical drugs after my doctor prescribed more than seven different medications for depression, anxiety, insomnia, chronic diarrhea (brought on by antidepressants), and high blood pressure. Within a few weeks of eating the mushrooms, I went off all my medications, including the blood pressure pills I had been taking for sixteen years. The shift in my mind was so dramatic, so life-changing, and so profound, I had to write this book.

During the three years following my mushroom healing, I spent two winters skiing in Lake Tahoe, two summers surfing in Mexico, did a lot of traveling, and had many ups and downs. The pandemic brought unprecedented, trying times but also made me understand the importance of breath work—a big part of my life now—and cultivating a resilient mind and a positive outlook on life. We have to stay physically healthy and remain present and in control if we're going to persevere through trying times. Now, more than ever, we need to reflect on our actions and raise our individual and collective awareness by looking inward to determine how we've manifested the world we live in and what we can do to reverse this crisis of consciousness.

I've learned throughout my journey that everything can be solved by transcending the limitations of the ego. All suffering and all depression is a product of the ego—an inherent and necessary part of our human existence. The trick is to get to know and befriend our ego, dominate it when necessary, and most importantly, learn to peacefully coexist with it. This book is my manual and blueprint for achieving that—the rules of engagement with my ego.

Depression is the leading cause of disability in the world. More than 3,000 people commit suicide every day. The mental health care industry has been stagnant for decades, unable to reverse this growing global epidemic, because its approach to this deeply misunderstood condition is all wrong. Contrary to popular Western belief, depression is not a disease. It is a symptom of several complex and multifaceted biological, psychological, nutritional, environmental, and societal factors, and taking harmful, addictive pharmaceutical drugs to try to suppress natural and necessary human emotions is not the answer. The opioid crisis is an obvious symptom of our inadequate mental health care system, as people turn to anything that is legally available to try to relieve their suffering.

It's time to change this paradigm and put science and human lives above politics. It's time to change the antiquated laws surrounding psychedelics. It's time to reawaken our incredible inner power and reconnect with nature. It's time to evolve.

IT WAS ALL A DREAM

"When we are no longer able to change a situation, we are challenged to change ourselves."
~ *Victor Frankl*

Nothing I could say or do would convince her to stay. She had been seeing another man. I begged. I pleaded. How could she? I worked so hard for years to provide the life of our dreams, an epic life on the white sand beaches of Playa del Carmen, Mexico. We had settled in Mexico after searching throughout Central America for our ideal home two years earlier. When we returned from our destination wedding in Roatan, Honduras, and our month-long honeymoon in Colombia in the spring of 2013, we couldn't quite assimilate back to our stressful, time-consuming jobs, so we saved our money, sold all our belongings, and moved south of the border to start a vacation rental business a year later. We rented a small apartment, simple but spacious, blocks from the turquoise waters of the Caribbean, and had lots of free time to enjoy life, living our dream.

How could she betray me after everything I'd done to make this happen? How could she ruthlessly discard me from the life we'd built together? How could she be so selfish? The more I spoke, the more distant she became. The louder I screamed, the less she could hear me. A violent rage came over me. I could not accept this; she had to pay for what she had done.

I pulled out the travel knife my brother had given me three years earlier, when my wife and I had started our journey and new life together in Central America, and slashed her face across her right eye, slicing it open. As blood splattered on my face and clothes, her face became distorted, eyes bulging, as her rapidly swelling head grew into a grotesque bloody balloon. I slashed again and again, anger and rage throbbing through my veins. She seemed oblivious to what was happening, unperturbed by my violent attack. What was happening? Was she not human? Was she some sort of demon? I slashed her face over and over, desperately seeking a reaction. Her head continued to swell. I felt a sudden sickness in my stomach and a feeling of utter sadness and loneliness.

I woke up in a cold sweat. It was 4:13 a.m. on March 9, 2018. The room was quiet and dark, the cold, brisk Lake Tahoe air blowing in through the window I had cracked open because the heater had been on overdrive when I laid down to sleep. I had fallen asleep to a particularly violent episode of "Vikings," a show my wife and I had loved binge watching together before everything fell apart, in which King Aelle executed Ragnar Lothbrok, slashing deep cuts on Ragnar's forehead with a large knife before throwing him into a pit of serpents. All Ragnar's achievements, failures, joys, and betrayals flashed through his head moments before death.

I felt the same sense of doom I'd had every day since she had walked out on me. Scared that depression's ugly head was back and looking for a fight, I laid in bed for the next hour, trying to fall back asleep, restless, empty, scared, with a loneliness deep in my gut. I decided to stop fighting myself and get up. Feeling more somber and alone than I had felt since eating magic mushrooms ten weeks prior, I sat for a moment in the dark, wondering where my life was headed, if I would fall back into depression, if I would ever meet anyone again, if I would die alone.

A month after my wife left me, two weeks after what would have been our fourth anniversary, my dad died. Instead of celebrating in a tropical paradise, drinking out of coconuts and diving into warm, clear waters, I spent our anniversary watching my dad's body shut down. A few weeks later, I found out I had developed otosclerosis, a rare hereditary condition in which the stapes bone in the middle ear calcifies and hardens, drastically reducing the transfer of sound to the inner ear. I was going deaf. My mind had taken a nosedive into the depths of hell. My condition required surgery that has a high success rate, but if it failed, I would completely lose my hearing. After losing my wife, my home, my business, my dad, and my desire to live, I couldn't stand the thought of losing my hearing, too. The world was growing darker every day.

It was my last day in Lake Tahoe. Three job prospects that had lured me back to this spectacular lake had fallen through, so I had no choice but to head back to my family in San Diego. My bank account had been dwindling since my wife's and my business had fallen victim to the dismantling of our shared life; it was the lowest it had been in the last decade. We had sold everything before we left for Panama four years earlier, so I had no car, and my phone was broken. I was hitching a ride with a friend who was driving through Lake Tahoe on his way to San Diego, and I was worried it would be a difficult day as I packed up my belongings to hit the road again on an uncertain path. Would my mind start racing and turn against me again? When I was in the depths of depression, I had struggled to simply lift my head off the pillow every morning, let alone get anything accomplished. I reached for a coin I'd bought for myself right after my mushroom journey a couple weeks earlier that said, "You could leave life right now." I read it a few times, clenched my fist tightly around it, opened the window to let the crisp, fresh mountain air hit my face, and told myself to begin, to trust the system I'd begun to develop to keep myself mentally and physically healthy.

I grabbed my mind-dump journal, scribbled down all my dark thoughts and worries, and set the journal aside. Next, I wrote down three things I was grateful for in my five-minute journal: I had a ride to San Diego with a good friend, a skiing buddy from high school; I was in Lake

Tahoe; I had my health, which, aside from potential hearing loss, was the best it had ever been. I asked myself how I could make the day awesome, struggled to think positively, and went back to the basics. I would smile, thank everyone I came across, and take a moment in nature. I then jotted down the same affirmation I had written every morning for the past two months: *I am ecstatic for what's coming.* Did I believe it? Not exactly, but I wrote it anyway, set the journal down, and felt a little lighter, a little more positive.

Time to get out of my head and into my body. I stood up and straightened out my posture. I had started a daily yoga routine the day after I arrived in Lake Tahoe and was noticing amazing results, both physically and mentally. I closed my eyes, placed my hands to heart center, and checked in with my body. I was a bit calmer than when I awoke, but not by much. A few poses facing the open window, fresh air blowing into the room, the pine trees swaying slowly outside the window with the beautiful blue lake illuminated by the rising sun. Hands back to heart center and down to the floor. Time to get high on my own supply. Deep breath. Belly, chest, head. Belly, chest, head. Belly, chest, head. My head felt light as I held my first retention breath. Two minutes passed, deep breath, hold. Fifteen seconds. Another deep breath. Belly, chest, head. Belly, chest, head. Three more cycles. Deep breath, hold for twenty seconds. I buzzed from head to toe as a complete wave of peacefulness and relaxation filled my entire body, all thoughts completely drowned out by the physical sensation of the breaths.

I forgot all about my soul-shattering nightmare as I lay for a minute, breathing slowly, deeply, evenly, feeling gratitude for this new ability to bring myself to peace. I opened my eyes and made my way to the shower, starting with a quick shock of cold water for thirty seconds before turning the water to hot and enjoying the soothing sensation of the hot water lulling me into a dreamlike state.

I turned the knob all the way to the coldest temperature, which in Lake Tahoe, is ice cold. Shock! Breathe! Twenty seconds later, it became tolerable and then felt warm. Sixty deep breaths later, I turned off the water, my entire body buzzing, feeling energized but relaxed, light, and alert. I stepped out of the shower and smiled at myself in the mirror, fully aware in the present moment.

My worries had washed away. I was looking forward to my journey to San Diego and the opportunities that awaited me. I felt genuinely happy and grateful to be alive, and I gave thanks to the universe for these gifts I had been forced to learn through intense pain and suffering—this routine I had practiced for the last three months was all I needed to navigate life's inevitable adversities. It was an antidote for the nightmares I would continue to have of my previous life in Mexico. I felt bulletproof.

DEPRESSION

Great Grief does not, of itself, put an end to itself.
~ Seneca

It started as a passionate, loving relationship and ended in a dysfunctional power struggle littered with hate.

My ex-wife and I had both grown up dealing with financial challenges and difficulties that had resulted in psychological issues for us as adults. Anger was a big one, and our union was one of intense passion and equally intense fighting. We were either having incredible adventures, like getting married barefoot on a stunning beach in the Bay Islands of Honduras, or in a full-blown meltdown, like the huge fight we had after a day of skiing in St. Anton, Austria, that caused us to lose our footing and slide hundreds of meters to the bottom of the mountain, yelling at each other the whole way. During another big fight when we were living and working on the island of Bastimentos in Bocas del Toro, Panama, she packed her bags, ready to hike through the jungle in the middle of the night to go back home. A friend intervened and stopped her alcohol-infused walk through the dense jungle full of caiman-infested lagoons.

We were a match made in both heaven and hell. When we weren't fighting, we were truly living the dream. The world was our oyster, and anything was possible. We could turn dreams into reality. But we were equally as good at breaking each other down, alienating, and destroying each other. We weathered the storms to preserve the dream, but every fight chipped away at our marriage's foundation. Living in paradise surrounded by friends, we shored up our crumbling marriage with parties and adventures. When we opened up shop in Mexico in the summer of 2016, I thought we had realized our dream.

For my fortieth birthday, my wife and my best friend—the one who had moved to Germany with me when we were nineteen—planned a surprise ski trip to Europe so he and I could retrace the magical circuit that changed my life and defined my early adulthood. On January 26, 2017, my friend and I flew from Cancun to Garmisch-Partenkirchen, Germany, a few days before my birthday, to spend the next three weeks skiing some of the biggest and best mountains on Earth. The trip was an epic adventure down memory lane, skiing the same mountains, eating at the same restaurants, hitting all the same bars and spots. Back home, business was good. I looked forward to returning home to Playa del Carmen, where I would work a few hours a week, ride my bike, relax on white sand beaches, paddleboard, dive into warm turquoise waters, snorkel with whale sharks, and swim in the cool cenotes under the lush Mayan jungle.

But when I landed in Cancun, I felt immediately that something was off. My wife and I had started having communication issues and hesitance shortly after our first anniversary, but something was different this time; she was especially distant. Within a day, we got into a nasty argument. "I can't do this anymore," she said.

We spent the next two weeks walking on eggshells. She stayed out late most nights with new friends, and my gut told me something was seriously wrong as we argued again and again. One night she went out with the girls and didn't come home. I stayed up all night, worried sick, texting and calling to no response. At 6 a.m., a strange car pulled up, and she emerged.

"How did you get home?" I demanded.

"I took a taxi," she said.

My heart sank. It was the worst moment I've ever experienced.

She packed up and moved out that morning, leaving

me alone in an empty apartment in Mexico, my life and my future demolished. I'd never felt so low or so lost, and I fell instantly into a soul-shattering depression, plagued by insomnia and nightmares. My blood pressure shot through the roof, and the diabetes I had managed for decades spun out of control.

I went home to spend a month with my family in Oceanside, the town north of San Diego where I'd grown up, too ashamed to tell anyone except my brother and sister that I was there. My brother did his best to help me through, but I struggled to have even a normal conversation. I couldn't focus and didn't want to see anyone. I was hiding out in my brother's apartment when we got the call from my other sister. Our dad had had a stroke. No. No. No.

The next ten months were the darkest days of my life. My dad fought for his life for ten days, unable to swallow and therefore no longer able to nourish or hydrate himself. I felt sanity slipping away as I tried to process my failed marriage while watching my dad's body shut down. He had an infectious personality and was loved by many, and family members I hadn't seen in years came to visit until his body finally gave up. I was the only member of my family who simply couldn't speak at the funeral.

A few weeks later, I went back to Playa del Carmen to pick up the rest of my belongings and dismantle our business and dreamy Caribbean life. On top of everything else, I was having trouble hearing, constantly straining to comprehend conversations. This was compounding my social isolation, as self-consciousness made it almost impossible to feel normal in social settings. My auditory senses were closing me off from the world just as my mind was giving up.

I made an appointment to get my hearing checked when I returned to San Diego and learned I'd lost about eighty percent of my hearing in both ears. I gave up. I had no fight left in me. The universe had decided my time was up, and I surrendered. I started drinking heavily, fully understanding—and welcoming—the repercussions of my risky behavior. I thought about how easy it would be to just end it all, how a few seconds of intense pain would be better than this life. My sister's apartment in Oceanside was just a block away from Amtrak tracks, but I could no longer hear the sound of trains barreling through town, a pervasive part of my childhood. Instead, I daydreamed about jumping in front of one.

Anyone who suffers severe depression knows the feeling of wanting to slip away in your sleep. The emptiness is hard to put into words. There's no light at the end of the tunnel, not even the dim flicker of a dying light bulb. As my life fell into this dark abyss, I saw four therapists over several months before giving up on therapy all together. Nothing anyone could say would change what had happened. After I broke into tears when my fourth therapist asked how I was doing, she recommended antidepressants before even hearing my story. My doctor prescribed Sertraline, the generic for Zoloft, which didn't help at all. After a slight lessening of emotion for about a week, my mind returned to darkness. The drug may even have contributed to my suicidal thoughts, as I learned later that's a side effect of many antidepressants—a ridiculous irony. I started having chronic diarrhea, and my insomnia worsened, but I was afraid to stop taking the pills because my life was on the brink of collapse.

My downward spiral continued for seven more months until I landed in jail in December of 2017. I was drinking my sorrows away when a bartender cut me off, and I got so angry that she got scared and called the police. Being locked up for the night barely phased me. I'd been expecting it, and I was certain the next stop would be the morgue. My family was desperate to help. A few days later, my brother suggested I try magic mushrooms.

LIBERATION

If the doors of perception were cleansed, everything would appear to man as it is: infinite.
~ William Blake

My experiments with psychedelics when I was in my twenties had been magical, but my life was much different when I was an adrenaline junkie and hardcore ski bum living life to the fullest in the German Alps. I hadn't experienced any major hardships and was having the time of my life. When my brother suggested I try eating mushrooms again twenty years later, my life was much different. I worried about being drawn deeper into my dark thoughts and depression. But I had to give it a shot.

On December 22, 2017, my brother came to the apartment early in the morning. We ate a small handful of mushrooms and took a walk on the beach as the sunrise illuminated the Pacific Ocean on a clear, cool winter morning. The glassy waves and the briny smell of the ocean lifted my mood a bit. By the time we reached the pier, a familiar nervous energy was flowing through me. I felt a bit scared, but it was too late to go back. I had to go with the flow, whatever that flow may be. If I knew one thing about psychedelics, it was the importance of surrendering to the experience because fighting it only makes it worse—an epiphany I would have later about life itself. By the time we were halfway down the pier, my nervous energy melted into euphoria, nostalgia, and comfort. The fear, sadness, hopelessness, and emptiness that had overwhelmed me since the day it all fell apart were gone.

I was admiring the dolphins frolicking in the distant water and the pelicans surfing the glassy waves in perfect choreography when it struck me that the ocean was bright blue—the color of home for me. For the past ten months, when I had looked out at the water from the couch in my sister's apartment, my mind had seen only gray. I'd lost the love for surfing I'd had since I was a small child, and I hadn't set foot in the water since I returned to Oceanside. The ocean had become a scary, gray abyss, just like my life and my mind. Every morning, I had walked to the pier so I could hide my tears from my family and pull myself together to deal with the day, returning to the apartment feeling lonely, empty, and utterly lost. As I basked in my beloved ocean's bright blue, I understood what it means to create your own reality. If my mind could strip the ocean of its color to match the darkness of my life, what else could it do? Confident that I was in for a good day, I forgot about my worries and began taking in everything and everyone around me.

We walked on the pier for about an hour and returned to the apartment as the mushrooms' magic took hold. Vibrating with energy and curiosity, my brother and I decided to go for a longer walk in the opposite direction—a simple decision, so refreshing after struggling every day with even the smallest ones, like what to eat for breakfast. We packed a day bag and walked out onto the sand, heading south. I'd grown up in Oceanside and spent most of my summers on this beach, but the thought of walking to Carlsbad had never crossed my mind. Why? It was so easy and so beautiful.

We slowly strolled barefoot in the sand, wading in the water, talking about life. After a few hours, I gave my mind permission to visit my marriage and think about what had happened from a different perspective, without sadness, regret, hate, rage, guilt, and fear. I easily acknowledged that both of us made choices and took actions that led our marriage to its inevitable end. The yin and yang of it all made perfect sense. Our childhood experiences had shaped how we dealt with conflict, and this was not inherently good or bad, right or wrong, or—most importantly—intentional. When I was afraid our marriage was crumbling, I tried to tighten the reins but instead pushed her away. She was just trying to survive; she simply wanted to feel loved. I saw and felt the true, natural love we had for each other underneath our defense mechanisms. We didn't hate each other; we simply didn't know how to guide our emotions to allow love to flourish. We both fell victim to the wrath of uncontrolled, untethered emotions.

I stopped hating her for what she'd done. I realized every misfortune I'd ever had was contingent on how I perceived life and reacted. I saw how my reactions create my reality, that I was responsible for every experience in my life. I suddenly felt in complete control, a feeling of empowerment I had lost. In which direction would I now steer this ship?

I decided then and there that I would take control of my emotions and my mind. The answer is always in the present moment, for that is the decision point for reactions. I had taped a quote from Viktor E. Frankl Austrian neurologist, psychiatrist, and Holocaust survivor, behind our bedroom door in Playa del Carmen when I was learning about meditation that sums this up perfectly: "Between a stimulus and response, there is a space. In that space is our power to choose our response. In our response lies our growth and our freedom." With the mushrooms' help, this quote—which I had understood conceptually—lodged in my brain as an undeniable truth. I could learn from the lesson being presented to me, or I could go back to the same destructive egoic thought patterns that were killing me.

The mushrooms scooped up all my dark, negative thoughts, fears, insecurities, hate, sadness, and anger and placed them in a closet for the day so I could notice the beauty around me— the soft sand, the cold shock of the ocean—free from their life-crushing grip. I was mesmerized by the dance of nature as pelicans soared smoothly overhead like they didn't have a care in the world, simply existing. One of the *dichos*, or funny sayings, my dad was known for was, *agusto como un pelicano* ("as comfortable as a pelican")—and they do always look comfortable, no matter what they're doing. I felt a deep connection to nature and the universe, tightly fused to everything around me.

My brother and I sat on the sand and watched the sun set into the ocean, painting sky and sea with brilliant hues of red and orange, a glow that pulsed through my mind. The sun dipped below the horizon, offering up a flash of green, sending blue and violet light scattering as it swallowed up the bright red and yellow. We weren't quite ready to end the day, so we strolled to a beach restaurant for food and perhaps a celebratory drink. As we settled down to relax at our table and start sipping our drinks, we heard a commotion outside, where people were yelling and pointing up at the sky. Not a dull moment today! We walked outside to see three fireballs screeching across the sky. What the heck?! Was it meteors? Aliens? People were animatedly making their best guesses as we stood in awe under this planetary spectacle. Someone found an explanation on their phone: SpaceX had just launched a Falcon 9 rocket from Vandenberg Air Force Base in Santa Barbara.

The electric energy in the crowd made it feel as if everyone were a part of our mushroom journey. The shared moment of freedom, breaking through barriers, hope, achievement, transcendence, exploration, and joy— all the things I'd given up on—was the perfect ending to a transformative day. After dinner, we hopped on the train and headed south to Solana Beach to meet my niece and her boyfriend. As we laughed and shared stories of our day, I felt again a joy I had long forgotten.

The next morning as the sun peeked in through the front door, the good vibes remained. I walked across the street to get a cup of coffee, then out to the pier, as I had for the past ten months—but this time, I was free of sorrow. I wasn't quite sure how I should feel now that I didn't feel sad. Quite the opposite, I felt optimistic and happy, free. The world around me felt crisp and clean, the air thick with positivity. I knew I no longer needed antidepressants, which had never helped me, anyway.

THE CASE FOR PSYCHEDELICS

The capacity of psychedelic drugs to exteriorize otherwise invisible phenomena and make them the subject of scientific investigation gives these substances a unique potential as research tools for the exploration of the human mind. It does not seem inappropriate or an exaggeration to compare their potential significance for psychiatry to that of the microscope for medicine or the telescope for astronomy.
~ *Stanislav Grof*

The first photograph of earth ever taken from space, called Blue Marble, was inspired by an LSD trip on a rooftop in San Francisco in the spring of 1966. Stewart Brand, an American writer best known as the editor of the *Whole Earth Catalog*, realized in the midst of his journey that the downtown streets were not parallel from his vantage point. That led him to muse that we had no photos of Earth from space and to wonder, if we did, whether people would realize just how finite Earth's resources are and be inspired to curb their consumption. Brand launched a campaign that eventually reached Congress and NASA, leading to that iconic Apollo photograph in 1968.[1]

But if you mention psychedelics to most people today, you are likely to get a response rooted in skepticism and apprehension, maybe a reference to the hippie 1960s. That's when political forces snuffed out any knowledge of and education about psychedelics, leaving us with urban myths and propaganda despite promising results from research that had been conducted for the previous two decades. Psychedelics faded from the practice of psychiatry and mental health in 1971 and didn't return until 1994. During those years, nearly all psychedelic research in the United States stopped, though a small group of advocates continued to work diligently to revive exploration of the human mind through psychedelics. It is thanks to these brave pioneers that we find ourselves in the midst of a psychedelic renaissance with resurrected hope of saving and improving lives and possibly liberating humanity from the prison of the ego.

Some of the best scientists in the world are now conducting cutting-edge psychedelic research at institutes such as the Centre for Psychedelic Research at Imperial College in London; the Center for Psychedelic and Consciousness Research at Johns Hopkins in Baltimore, Maryland; New York University; University of Los Angeles, California; and U.C.-Berkeley Center for the Science of Psychedelics. With $6.4 million in private funding, the University of California-San Francisco (UCSF) founded the Neuroscape Psychedelics Division, a multidisciplinary research center that bridges the gap between neuroscience and technology.

"Our generous funders are making possible a major leap forward in generating evidence of clinical efficacy and safety for individuals using psychedelics to treat a broad range of mental health conditions, including depression, anxiety, PTSD, and addiction," said Executive Director Adam Gazzaley. "At Neuroscape, we have taken a neuroscience-based, closed-loop approach to creating experiential medicine." Robin Carhart-Harris, one of the world's most-cited researchers in psychedelic science and the founder of the first center for psychedelic research at Imperial College London, is Neuroscape's founding director. "The founding of this new division is a hugely exciting development in the story of the psychedelic renaissance," he said.[2]

Drug Science, an international scientific committee founded in the United Kingdom by Professor David Nutt, a leading pioneer and expert in the psychedelic renaissance, is a completely independent, science-led charity that's bringing together leading drug experts from a wide range of expertise and disciplines to carry out ground-breaking research into harms and effects.[3] Mind Medicine Australia was founded by Tania de Jong and Peter Hunt to help alleviate the suffering caused by mental illness in Australia by expanding the treatment options available to medical practitioners and their patients. Operating as a nexus between medical practitioners, academia, government, regulatory bodies, philanthropists, and other partners, Mind Medicine Australia focuses specifically on the clinical application of medicinal psilocybin and medicinal MDMA for certain mental illnesses.[4] The Multidisciplinary Association for Psychedelic Studies (MAPS), founded by Rick Doblin in 1986, is conducting a "randomized, double-blind, placebo-controlled, multi-site phase 3 study of the efficacy and safety of manualized MDMA-assisted therapy for the treatment of severe post-traumatic stress disorder" at fifteen research sites in the U.S., Canada, and Israel.[5] MAPS is also initiating phase 2 trials in Europe.

No one in recorded history has ever died directly from LSD or psilocybin mushrooms. It is virtually impossible to overdose on most of the "classic psychedelics" (psilocybin, LSD, DMT, and mescaline). If we wish to dispel the ubiquitous misconceptions surrounding psychedelics, we must understand their history.

The word "psychedelic," from the Greek words "psyche" (mind) and "delos" (manifesting), wasn't the applied term for this class of drugs until 1957. LSD was introduced to psychiatry in the early 1950s as LSD-25, short for Lysergic Acid Diethylamide. It was the twenty-fifth molecule Albert Hoffman, a chemist working for Sandoz Laboratories in Switzerland in 1938, isolated from ergot, a fungus fermented from rye grain, when he was searching for a marketable drug to help induce labor in women during childbirth. LSD-25 was classified as a psychotomimetic, a type of drug that induces effects that resemble psychosis. Over the years, LSD along with MDMA, mescaline, psilocybin, and dimethyltryptamine (DMT) became known as psychedelics.[6]

For two decades after LSD's discovery, psychedelics were studied as a treatment for addiction, depression, obsessive-compulsive disorder, schizophrenia, autism, and end-of-life anxiety. More than 1,000 clinical papers with over 40,000 research participants were published in the 1940s and 1950s, and the American Psychiatric Association conducted several meetings to discuss LSD's scientific potential.[7] But the rise of neurochemistry in the 1950s led to the discovery of serotonin, which then led to the development of selective serotonin reuptake inhibitors (SSRIs), which usurped psychedelics to become the most common type of antidepressants used today.[8]

In the 1950s, the Central Intelligence Agency began looking into LSD as a possible truth serum, mind-control agent, or chemical weapon, conducting research through its classified MK-Ultra mind-control program, created and run by American chemist Sidney Gottlieb. The CIA was interested in weaponizing LSD to "get control of an individual to the point where he will do our bidding against his will and even against fundamental laws of nature, such as self-preservation?"[9] Gottlieb convinced the CIA to pay $240,000 to buy the world's entire supply of LSD. Some of his experiments were covertly funded at universities and research centers, others conducted in American prisons and detention centers in Germany, Japan, and the Philippines. Many involved psychological torture such as trying to break subjects by making them endure electroshock, extreme temperatures, and sensory isolation while on heavy doses of LSD. Whitey Bulger, a prisoner who volunteered for what he was told was an experiment to find a cure for schizophrenia, was given LSD daily for more than a year before he learned the real objective was to find out whether long-term use would cause a person to lose their mind. Many subjects died.[10]

In 1960, the CIA paid hundreds of volunteers to try LSD as a part of its research at the Menlo Park Veterans Hospital in California. In a turn of events the CIA could not have possibly imagined, some of the volunteers' experiences led to the movement that ultimately brought MK-Ultra and the Vietnam War to its demise. Ken Kesey, the author of *One Flew Over the Cuckoo's Nest*, was so influenced by his experience that he handed out thousands of LSD doses in San Francisco to "change the mind of a generation," as he put it, turning people against the war. After Sandoz stopped producing and distributing LSD in 1965, stating that it had become "a serious threat to public health" in some parts of the world,[11] Augustus Owsley Stanley, the soundman for the Grateful Dead and a clandestine chemist, began manufacturing and distributing it illegally. Grateful Dead lyricist Robert Hunter and poet Allen Ginsberg were among the counterculture luminaries inspired by the drug.

In 1955, Gordon Wasson, vice president of public relations for J.P. Morgan, traveled to Huautla de Jiménez in Oaxaca, Mexico, and became the first Westerner in recorded history to eat the mushrooms ancient Aztecs called *teonanácatl*, which means "flesh of the gods" in their native language. Following the Spanish conquest, the Roman Catholic Church had brutally repressed anyone who used the sacred mushrooms because it considered them a threat to the church's authority,[12] but the Mazatec people continued to use them in a healing ritual known as a *velada*. Maria Sabina, a Mazatec *curandera*, allowed Wasson to experience a *velada*, and he wrote about it in a famous article, "Seeking the Magic Mushroom," for *Life* magazine and shared his firsthand account on the popular CBS program, "Person to Person." In 1958, Wasson sent mushroom specimens to LSD inventor Albert Hoffman, who isolated and synthesized psilocybin and psilocin, adding it to a growing list of psychedelic compounds.[13]

Wasson's description of the mushrooms that caused

strange visions sparked a wave of musicians, artists, poets, and hippies—including John Lennon, Mick Jagger, and Bob Dylan—to descend on the sleepy mountain village of Huautla de Jimenez, shattering the village and causing Sabina to regret giving Wasson a taste. "The saint children (the mushrooms) lost their purity," she said. "They lost their force; the foreigners spoiled them." Wasson also regretted publicizing his visit as he watched "a torrent of commercial exploitation of the vilest kind" transform Huautla. All the attention attracted the Mexican police, completely changing the social dynamics of the Mazatec village and threatening their ancient healing custom. The village blamed Sabina, burned her house down, and even put her in jail.

In 1960, Timothy Leary, a charismatic and flamboyant Harvard University psychologist, had his own life-changing experience with the mushrooms in Cuernavaca, Mexico. He began conducting psilocybin research at Harvard and became a vocal advocate for psilocybin and LSD. He told Americans to "tune in, turn on, and drop out," inspiring a wave of youth to drop out of school and thousands to refuse to fight in Vietnam. Over the next decade, the counterculture's opposition to authority and institutions grew, largely through music and art. People were brought together with an expanded awareness and a common goal, transmuting LSD from a tool for war to a proliferation of love, music, and art. The government had to do something.

President Richard Nixon declared Leary "the most dangerous man in America" in 1971, and LSD was classified as a Schedule 1 drug, meaning it had no accepted medical use and a high potential for abuse. This politically motivated move had nothing to do with science or health, but a wave of panic about mind-altering drugs, fueled by the media, spread throughout the country and the world. Research into the healing power of psychedelics was halted and its archives locked up until 1994, when

University of New Mexico psychiatrist Rick Strassman received government approval to research the physiological effects of dimethyltryptamine (DMT), a powerful psychedelic molecule ubiquitous in nature. The genie was back out of the bottle.

In 2006, the Supreme Court reinstated Native Americans' right to use mescaline, a psychedelic molecule in the peyote cactus, as a sacrament in their ceremonies, as they had done for generations, under the First Amendment's religious freedom clause. This opened the door for the União do Vegetal (UDV), a Christian spiritist sect founded in Brazil in 1961, to start importing ayahuasca, which contains the Schedule 1 substance DMT, into the United States.[14] Since then, extensive research has been done with LSD, psilocybin, DMT, methylenedioxy methamphetamine (MDMA, also known as ecstasy), and more recently, ibogaine and ketamine to treat depression, addiction, PTSD, anxiety, and mental disorders, replicating many of the promising results from the first wave of psychedelic research in the 1950s and 1960s with remarkably low toxicity levels.

Psilocybin has been found to decrease alcohol cravings,[15] help people stop smoking,[16] and lower odds of opiate use disorder.[17] A 2011 clinical trial at Johns Hopkins showed that a single psilocybin session could give people a more open personality, greater appreciation for new experiences, and enhanced curiosity and imagination,[18] or what Bob Jesse, a computer engineer turned psychedelic enthusiast, calls the "betterment of well people."[19] Psilocybin has been used successfully to treat end-of-life anxiety in about 80 percent of terminally ill cancer patients in one session, with virtually no side effects.[20] In 2022, researchers found that psilocybin therapy changes brain patterns associated with depression and reduces depression symptoms.[21] In another clinical trial, 61 percent of 107 participants no longer had PTSD symptoms two months after MDMA-assisted psychotherapy. In light of these findings, the FDA recently deemed MDMA and psilocybin "breakthrough therapies," putting them on the fast track for approval.[22]

Thanks to new brain-imaging technologies like functional magnetic resonance imaging (fMRI) and magnetoencephalography (MEG), technologies that didn't exist during the first wave of research in the 1950s and 1960s. Scientists are now able to observe the biological processes occurring in the brain under the influence of psychedelics. What we're learning is as mind-blowing as the molecules themselves.

LSD, psilocybin, mescaline, and DMT (collectively known as the "classic psychedelics") are organic compounds called tryptamines found in plants, fungi, and animals. Serotonin (5-hydroxytryptamine), an important neurotransmitter in the brain and body that modulates cognition, reward, learning, memory, and numerous other physiological processes like circadian rhythm, which is important for sleep regulation, is also a tryptamine. Depleted serotonin levels are thought to play a role in depression as well as insomnia. When a tryptamine is ingested, it mimics serotonin closely enough that it binds with the serotonin receptor $5\text{-}HT_{2a}$,[23] found in large numbers in the outermost part of the human brain, the cortex. LSD actually has a stronger affinity for the receptor than serotonin itself.[24]

In 2001, Washington University neurologist Marcus Raichle was establishing the baseline setting for fMRI experiments when he stumbled upon the default mode network (DMN), which he later described as "the area of the brain which increases in activity during its resting state."[25] When the mind is idling with no specific tasks to perform, the DMN turns on and starts daydreaming, ruminating, time traveling, self-reflecting, and worrying.

The DMN is also the area of the brain that creates mental constructions, such as our sense of self that Eastern philosophies and psychologists call the ego. Raichle had established, for the first time in history, the neural correlates that activate the ego.

Carhart-Harris describes the DMN as a traffic control center for mostly independent, specialized areas of the brain that normally don't communicate so signals don't get mixed during conscious awareness. Carhart-Harris describes human consciousness as split into two parts: primary consciousness, driven by primitive areas of the brain such as the limbic system in the brain stem, and secondary consciousness, driven by the prefrontal cortex. "Primary consciousness is associated with beliefs about the world that have been shaped by wishes and fears and supernatural interpretation, while secondary consciousness pays deference to reality and diligently seeks to represent the world as precisely as possible in order to minimize surprise and uncertainty," he writes.[26]

The DMN is the superconductor between primary consciousness, which is responsible for creative thinking as well as processing fear and emotions, and the secondary consciousness, which contributes to more narrow, rigid thinking, obsessive-compulsive behavior, and addictive personalities, and acts as a filtering mechanism during normal waking consciousness. Without it, the influx of stimuli would overwhelm our senses and make it impossible to function. Evolution has refined this filtering device to become as fast and efficient as possible, minimizing the energy needed to exist. Using experience and memory to refine the system, the brain takes in as little sensory information as possible to formulate our reality.

The DMN doesn't begin to form until late childhood, after we've gathered some experience. As we age and get more experience under our belts, it starts making faster predictions so that by the time we're adults, our brain decodes what we're looking at faster than our sensory apparatus can confirm it. The result is what we call "reality"—actually more of a learned, habitual hallucination.[27] Without the DMN, young children look out at the world and see infinite possibilities and infinite realities as they test the waters of their new existence. Their brains are sponges, built for learning and adapting to the current environment, which requires paying attention to the present moment. As they gain experience over the years, their hypotheses get tested, realities get narrowed, consequences are learned and absorbed, and their sense of self begins to develop. By the time they reach adolescence, their sense of self is strong enough to develop an identity and the DMN takes over, making their thinking more rigid and narrow until one day they don't know how to operate the technology of the time. The brain's priority at this point is to avoid learned mistakes, and it's very good at analyzing, recording experiences, and learning from them but also very effective at sabotaging itself and overcomplicating things.

An example of this is how teenage climate activist Greta Thunberg views climate change and how a world run by adults can't seem to solve the crisis. As Greta said in her 2018 Ted Talk, she sees the issue as black and white. "I remember thinking it was very strange that humans, who are an animal species, among others, could be capable of changing the earth's climate, because if we were, and if it was really happening, we wouldn't be talking about anything else. As soon as you turn on the TV, everything would be about that. Headlines, radio, newspapers. You would never read or hear about anything else. As if there was a world war going on."

Perhaps our societal DMN has hardened beyond our ability to solve this existential threat bearing down on us. Yet somehow, we managed to rally the world to take the type of radical and abrupt action Thunberg has been fighting for when Covid hit. "If one virus can wipe out the entire economy in a matter of weeks, and shut down societies, then that is proof that our societies are not very resilient,"[28] Thunberg pointed out. "It also shows that once we are in an emergency, we can act, and we can change our behavior quickly." Can humanity only take drastic measures if the danger is right in front of us? Could psychedelics, yoga and meditation help us shift away from our DMN-centric civilization to understand the extreme urgency of the climate crisis?

If and when we can slow down the DMN, we can find "flow state," the term used to describe the state of heightened immersion experienced during meditation, exercise, sports, dancing, or creating art or music, among many other activities. Mihaly Csikszentmihalyi, the former chairman of the University of Chicago Department of Psychology, described this as "an expansion of self, a sense of unity, and meaningfulness in life" that "lingers in one's consciousness and gives a sense of purpose, integration, self-determination, and empathy." During flow state, awareness of time, space, and personal needs diminishes,[29] and we feel we are exactly where we are supposed to be, doing exactly what we are supposed to be doing. The brain is so involved in the task at hand that there is no room for the mind to wander, time travel, or self-reflect—all mechanisms of the ego. The DMN has no purpose; there is no need for the ego's story. I experience this when I ski, surf, and rock climb, as adrenaline rushing through my veins ensures optimal focus. Perhaps this is why I love adventure sports so much; they free me from ego, if only temporarily.

In *Stealing Fire: How Silicon Valley, the Navy SEALS and Maverick Scientists are Revolutionizing the Way We Live and Work*, Steven Kotler and Jamie Wheal explain that six powerful neurotransmitters, which are also our pleasure chemicals—norepinephrine, dopamine, endorphins, serotonin, anandamide, and oxytocin—activate in varying sequences and concentrations during flow state, one of the only times all these chemicals get activated at once.[30] This "lifts the course of life to another level," Csikszentmihalyi writes in *Flow: The Psychology of Optimal Experience.*[31] "Alienation gives way to involvement, enjoyment replaces boredom, helplessness turns into a feeling of control. ... When experience is intrinsically rewarding, life is justified."

An fMRI study conducted on jazz musicians in 2008 found a reduction in DMN activity very similar to a child's brain or the brain of an adult during a psychedelic experience or in deep meditation.[32] Carhart-Harris found that volunteers injected with LSD and psilocybin showed a decrease in blood flow to the DMN and an increase in blood flow to the rest of the brain as they reported transcendence of self and ego dissolution.[33] When blood flow and electrical activity in the DMN are reduced, the brain becomes more globally connected, allowing areas that normally don't communicate with each other—such as the visual cortex and the amygdala, which processes fear and emotion—to connect. This can cause synesthesia, a mixing of the senses (tasting colors or seeing sounds), reemergence of forgotten or repressed memories, and hallucinations as the brain searches through its memories trying to make sense of its current reality. Hallucinations, essentially, allow the brain to create new perspectives and construct a new reality. This is what happened when I reflected on what I had perceived as the destruction of my life during that magical beach walk.

Carhart-Harris believes depression, addiction, and obsessive-compulsive disorders stem from "an excess of order" in secondary consciousness. As Michael Pollan writes in *How to Change Your Mind*, "When the grooves of self-reflective thinking deepen and harden, the ego becomes overbearing. This is most clearly evident in depression, when the ego turns on itself and uncontrollable introspection gradually shades out reality. We begin to see a reality shaped by the ego, sometimes called depressive realism."[34] This could be the result of an overactive DMN, which "traps us in repetitive and destructive loops of rumination that eventually close us off from the outside world," Pollan explains.

Carhart-Harris says people suffering from psychological disorders "can benefit from the ability of psychedelics to disrupt stereotyped patterns of thought and behavior by disintegrating the patterns of neural activity upon which they rest."[35] By silencing the DMN, "psychedelics loosen the ego's grip on the mind, refreshing perspective and jolting the mind out of its repetitive patterns." The brain activity of a child is very similar to an adult brain on psychedelics and during deep meditation, resulting in a sense of awe: the trees look new, the flowers are bright, the ocean turns bright blue. This is the product of our preconceptions being wiped away temporarily. A psychedelic experience, in essence, reverts our mind back to its childhood state, eager to observe, explore, learn, and wonder—the perfect antidote for a midlife crisis.

While I was under the influence of psilocybin, hundreds, if not thousands, of events leading up to my divorce scrolled through my mind and became neutral, devoid of positive, negative, or any duality of any kind. The self/other, subject/object duality dissipated, and I was able to see it all as life unfolding naturally, devoid of opinion or emotion, an inextricable part of the beauty of life—unpredictable, uncontrollable, vast. Life became beautiful again, and best of all, it made perfect sense. I was flooded with epiphanies every day for the next several months as I experimented with microdosing psilocybin. Scientists still don't understand why these effects seem to remain in the mind for weeks, months, and sometimes even years, but more often than not, the experience lingers for quite some time and, in therapeutic applications, leads to profound life changes. Though I was not in what would be considered a "therapeutic setting," the beach has always been my home and where I feel most comfortable, so it was the best therapeutic "setting" I could have asked for.

Shortly after Carhart-Harris published "Neural Correlates of the Psychedelic State as Determined by fMRI Studies with Psilocybin," Yale researcher Judson Brewer, using fMRI to study the brains of experienced meditators, also found that blood flow to the DMN drops during perceived transcendence of self.[36] As my own meditation practice has evolved over the course of this journey, I can attest that a deep meditative state feels very similar to my psychedelic experiences—a sense of oneness with the universe and transcendence of self. Our sense of self, or ego, inherently fosters the opposite: a feeling of separateness and isolation from other people and the universe itself, which shrinks our subjective universe. Roman emperor and Stoic philosopher Marcus Aurelius understood this thousands of years ago. "Meditate often on the interconnectedness and mutual interdependence of all things in the universe," he advised. "For in a sense, all things are mutually woven together and therefore have an affinity for each other, for one thing follows after another according to their tension of movement, their sympathetic stirrings, and the unity of all substance." This quote is my mantra, the unshakable truth I feel in my bones.

So, what is the common denominator in all this? The present moment. Our autobiographical memory creates our life story from past failures and fears of the future as it applies meaning to our experiences. It is said that if you suffer from depression, you are living in the past, and if you suffer from anxiety, you are living in the future. Most of us toggle back and forth between these two, something Buddhists have been aware of for thousands of years. In *The Power of Now*, Eckhart Tolle's message to the world is that mental freedom lives in the present moment.

American musician and artist Daniel Higgs says, "Anything other than the present moment is a form of slavery."

If we wish to live in this blissful, present moment, we must learn the concept of thoughtless awareness, observing and accepting life as it unfolds. This is when the beauty of the universe starts unfolding at our feet and we start noticing the miracles of life and the opportunities before us, so effectively blinded by the ego. By eliminating rumination and time travel, we can actually see what is happening now. Tolle writes that we must "surrender to what is," for there is only one way the world exists in the present moment. How we perceive it and what meaning we give it is up to us. Our distress is caused by wishing things could be different than they actually are, and that is impossible. We wish we weren't stuck in traffic or we had more money so we could buy a bigger house. I used to wish I was still married and my father was still alive. This was all resistance to what is. Meditation, yoga, psychedelics, art, and sports have helped me quiet my DMN, transcend my ego, and achieve presence and acceptance of what is. This is the key to happiness.

Science is finally overcoming propaganda and irrational fear, and we're now in the midst of a psychedelic renaissance. While certain psychedelics are legal or decriminalized in several countries, including Portugal, where all drugs were decriminalized in July 2001, the U.S. federal government still considers psychedelics Schedule 1 substances in the United States. But times are changing. Some states and municipalities are taking matters into their own hands.

On May 7, 2019, Denver became the first city in the United States to decriminalize psilocybin mushrooms, a landmark victory in a decades-long battle against prohibition.[37] Oakland and Santa Cruz quickly followed with decriminalization of all entheogens, a class of psychoactive substances, usually derived from plants and fungi, that induce a spiritual experience aimed at self-development or sacred use. In 2020, the Ann Arbor, Michigan, City Council voted unanimously to declare the investigation or arrest of anyone for planting, cultivating, purchasing, transporting, distributing, engaging in practices with, or possessing entheogenic plants or plant compounds to be the city's lowest law enforcement priority.[38]

That same year, voters made Oregon the first U.S. state to decriminalize psilocybin and legalize it for therapeutic use while decriminalizing all drugs across the state—a giant milestone in the failed war on drugs, essentially making drug use a social health issue as opposed to a criminal matter.[39] Also in 2020, voters in the District of Columbia passed the Entheogenic Plant and Fungus Policy Act, making arrests for possession or use of psilocybin, ayahuasca, and mescaline the lowest priority for D.C. police.[40] Washtenaw County, Michigan, followed suit in January 2021,[41] the same month the Somerville, Massachusetts, City Council voted unanimously to decriminalize possession of entheogenic plants, including psilocybin mushrooms and ibogaine.[42] The City Councils of Cambridge and Northampton, Massachusetts, soon followed suit.[43]

Across the United States, decriminalization efforts are underway as nearly 100 U.S. cities consider measures to decriminalize psilocybin or all entheogens. In 2019, Iowa state lawmaker Jeff Shipley introduced two bills that would legalize medical psilocybin and remove the drug from the state's list of controlled substances.[44] In 2020, four Vermont state lawmakers introduced a bill to decriminalize psilocybin, peyote, ayahuasca, and kratom,[45] New York Assemblywoman Linda Rosenthal introduced a decriminalization bill,[46] and a New Jersey senator added an amendment to a cannabis legalization bill that would decriminalize up to one ounce of psilocybin.[47] In 2021, California Senator Scott Weiner introduced Senate Bill 519, which would legalize psilocybin, psilocyn, MDMA, LSD, ketamine, DMT, ibogaine, and mescaline. The bill did not include peyote for conservation and cultural reasons.[48]

At the federal level, U.S. Representative Alexandria Ocasio-Cortez, a Democrat from New York, introduced an amendment to a spending bill to remove a budget rider inhibiting research into potential medical benefits of psychedelics in 2019 that was rejected in a floor vote. Ocasio-Cortez also called for decriminalization of psychedelics for personal use and later broadened that to include all illicit drugs.[49]

Exciting times. The wheels of progress are moving fast, and the wave is growing. Talking about this with your family, friends, and neighbors will raise awareness and help eliminate the societal fear surrounding these life-saving molecules, spread science, and erase lies.

That said, we can't always wait for the government to do the right thing. Had I done that, I would be dead. I do not believe it's unethical to take your health into your own hands. While I cannot condone illegal activity of any kind, there are resources out there to help people whose lives are clinging by a thread, as mine was. If you have the means, you can visit countries where the laws are more favorable to accessing these therapies, or you could access legally sanctioned clinical trials being conducted in the United States. Legal ayahuasca "churches," where entheogen use is decriminalized, are popping up across the country.

I must emphasize that responsible, therapeutic use of these molecules, not recreational use, must be the focus. An experienced guide and proper "set and setting," the psychological, social, and cultural parameters that shape a psychedelic experience, are imperative. The resources listed at the end of this book may be of help.

ADDICTION

God, grant me the serenity to accept the things I cannot change,
courage to change the things I can,
and wisdom to know the difference.
~ The Serenity Prayer

The Serenity Prayer, which is attributed to American theologian Reinhold Niebuhr, has been a hallmark of Alcoholics Anonymous (AA) since the organization's early days. AA co-founder Bill Wilson originally adapted the phrase to read: "Father, give us courage to change what must be altered, serenity to accept what cannot be helped, and the insight to know one from the other," but later simplified it.[50] The prayer has evolved to suggest that seeking a higher power will help people attain sobriety, which works in some cases but inadvertently deceives addicts into giving away their inner power to a dogmatic belief—to look for answers outside instead of inside ourselves.

There is debate about the prayer's philosophical origins, but no one will deny its striking similarities to many passages found in ancient Greek Stoic philosophy, a philosophy that has had a profound influence on my well-being since I stumbled across it just days after my psychedelic experience. Stoic philosopher Epictetus, a former slave, said 2,000 years ago, "Make the best use of what is in your power and take the rest as it happens. Some things are up to us, and some things are not up to us. Our opinions are up to us and our impulses, desires, aversions—in short, whatever is our own doing. Our bodies are not up to us, nor are our possessions, our reputations, or our public offices, or, that is, whatever is not our own doing."[51]

This is one of the main tenets of Stoic philosophy: identify what is in our control and what is not so we can solely focus on the former, wasting no time or energy trying to change things we cannot change. By eliminating wasted time and energy on things outside our control—most things—we can reallocate that time and energy for what we can control: our thoughts, actions, and dispositions. I do believe this philosophy can help an addict achieve sobriety.

Is this realistic, though? Can anyone simply adopt this new way of thinking? One problem I've had with the Serenity Prayer, despite its logical eloquence, is the first word, God. I find religion unappealing, and I'm suspicious of the idea that religion is the only route to sobriety. But studying the history of psychedelics is what led me to AA.

Before he co-founded AA, Wilson had a psychedelic, plant-derived alkaloid called belladonna administered to him at Town's Hospital in Manhattan in 1934. This experience was so profound and spiritually awakening that it sobered him up, and he co-founded AA a year later with another struggling alcoholic, Dr. Bob Smith, in Akron, Ohio.[52] Eight years later, Albert Hoffman first synthesized LSD, which was used to treat alcoholics at UCLA and Canada's Saskatchewan Province two decades later.

When this research on LSD and addiction surfaced, Wilson flew to Los Angeles to see if it offered a similar experience to the belladonna he had taken. Wilson tried LSD a few times with Sidney Cohen, an internist at Brentwood VA Hospital, and at UCLA, where a hub of LSD researchers was collaborating with around a dozen other such hubs in North America and Europe.[53] Wilson became so convinced that "LSD could reliably occasion the kind of spiritual awakening one needed in order to get sober" that he tried implementing it into AA therapy. His colleagues strongly disagreed, however, stating that "to condone the use of any mind-altering substance risked muddying the organization's brand and message."[54]

Understanding that the concept of surrendering to a "higher power," the backbone of AA and the twelve steps, was born out of Wilson's psychedelic experience makes the dogmatic approach unnecessary. Achieving transcendence by utilizing our own power through a variety of practices, disciplines, philosophies, and molecules makes sobriety more achievable, regardless of spiritual faith. It's unfortunate that LSD was not introduced into AA therapy. Current research on LSD treatment for alcoholism shows an 80 percent success rate for lasting alcohol abstinence, whereas the average success rate for alcohol cessation for people who attend at least one AA meeting ranges anywhere from 8 percent to 50 percent, depending on the origin of the studies (which are controversial because they're based on anecdotal information).[55] It is indisputable that psychedelics such as LSD, psilocybin, mescaline, and ibogaine are proving an effective—and safe--treatment for alcoholism and other addictions.

Unlike alcohol, psychedelics have never been attributed to any fatalities. Only a few cases of what would be considered an "overdose" of psychedelics have been documented, and though the experiences were intense and terrifying, the people who overdosed suffered no long-term damage—in fact, quite the opposite. These experiences resulted in miraculous, positive, and lasting physical and psychological effects.

In one case, a forty-six-year-old woman snorted a staggering 550 times the normal recreational dose of LSD (100 micrograms), thinking it was cocaine. She not only survived, but came out of the experience with drastically diminished foot pain, which she had suffered since she had contracted Lyme disease in her twenties. She was able to wean off the morphine she had been taking with no withdrawal symptoms. In another case, a fifteen-year-old girl with bipolar disorder accidentally took ten times the normal dose of LSD after the person who supplied her with liquid LSD made a decimal point error, giving her 1,000 mcg instead of 100 mcg. She had suffered from depression and hallucinations, which at times had landed her in the hospital, since she was twelve years old. After she overdosed, witnesses said she behaved erratically for six-and-a-half hours, then had a seizure as she lay in a fetal position with her arms and fists clenched tightly. An ambulance was called, but by the time the paramedics arrived, she was alert and oriented. The incident caused massive improvement in her mental health. When her father visited her in the hospital the next morning, she told him, "It's over." He thought she was referring to the LSD overdose, but she later clarified her bipolar illness was cured. She said she felt able to "experience life with a normal brain," free from all mental illness symptoms (bipolar or other) for the next thirteen years, until she gave birth and experienced postpartum depression.

These case reports were published in *the Journal of Studies on Alcohol and Drugs,* and the authors noted that it is impossible to conduct clinical trial research with dosages so high. " Professor David Nutt, director of the Neuropsychopharmacology Unit in the Division of Brain Sciences at Imperial College, London, said the cases "show that in some people, exceptionally high doses don't lead to enduring harms and may do some good."[56]

So, why do we prohibit molecules that have shown such a high success rate in ending addictions and have led to no direct fatalities while we blatantly promote alcohol, the third-most addictive substance after cocaine and heroin? Alcohol kills over 88,000 people per year in the United States alone.[57][58] In 2019, more than 7 percent of the US population, nearly 13.8 million Americans eighteen and older, suffered from alcohol addiction.[59] Scientific evidence of the negative and destructive effects of alcohol is endless. Just one alcoholic drink alters the structure and function of neurons in the dorsomedial striatum, the area of the brain that controls motivation and reward systems, which is why it's so hard to have just one drink. After that first drink, the shape of these neurons literally changes, urging you to order another round to keep up the buzz. We have created and normalized a drug with an instant withdrawal. Even worse, with prolonged consumption of alcohol, these changes become permanent on a structural level, making you forever crave that dirty martini.[60]

These statistics are widely known in the scientific community, yet alcohol is legal and ubiquitous in our society, promoted in every corner of our world. This is important to put into perspective when our conditioned fear of psychedelics arises and when we hear politicians argue against legalizing psychedelics. The question must be raised: just how much does society blind us from reality?

Psychedelics are effective in treating addiction because they trigger a deep-felt connection to everyone and everything around us, to the entire universe. In his powerful Ted Talk about addiction, Johann Hari says that the opposite of addiction is not sobriety, but connection.[61] This is illustrated in a famous experiment conducted in the early 1970s by Bruce Alexander, a psychology professor in British Columbia, replicated an experiment conducted in the 1920s in which rats were placed in empty cages with two water bottles, one laced with cocaine and one without, and overwhelmingly chose to drink the cocaine water, leading them to overdose and die.

Alexander's experiment had an important difference. He placed the rats in a cage with cheese, colorful balls, tunnels, and most importantly, plenty of rats of both sexes. The results were the exact opposite. The rats were not interested in the cocaine water at all. They rarely drank from it, and none of them drank it compulsively; no rats overdosed. This led Alexander to hypothesize that addiction isn't about the molecules but rather about the cage. This applies to humans as well.

Peter Cohen, a professor in the Netherlands, suggests addiction is actually our innate human need to bond. He believes happy, healthy humans bond easily with other humans and society but have a harder time connecting when they're traumatized. We bond instead with anything that brings relief, our relationship to the vice becoming more and more important as we reinforce our dependence on it. (Our deep need for connection is why Facebook took the world by storm. Every time we receive a like on our feed, we get a small hit of dopamine.) Conversely, Canadian addiction and trauma expert Dr. Gabor Mate believes loss of connection leads to loss of self, which is the source of our traumas. In his powerful 2021 documentary, *The Wisdom of Trauma*, Gabor says, "Addiction is a normal response to trauma. If someone is suffering, they're going to want to escape their suffering. That's normal."

Portugal, which had one of the worst drug problems in all of Europe, recognized this and took a bold step in 2001. After gathering several of Portugal's top scientists to approach the country's drug problem from a different angle, the government decriminalized all drugs. Twenty-one years later, the results are astonishing. Addiction on every metric, as well as HIV and suicides, have all dropped dramatically. It cannot be overlooked that Portugal used all the money it had spent enforcing prohibition to start a massive program of job creation for addicts and micro-loans for addicts to start small businesses. This helps assimilate addicts back into society, giving them another reason to get up in the morning. [62] Portugal should be a model for the rest of the world to follow.

THE WIM HOF METHOD

Breathe, motherfucker!! ~ *Wim Hof*

Seven months after my life fell apart, I was losing my mind and my grip on reality. I had chronic insomnia. I'd quit therapy after my fourth therapist failed to lift my spirits. The antidepressants were not working.

Meet-up groups were a temporary distraction. At one of them, a meditation group, the coordinator mentioned that she was a hypnotist and practiced something called "quantum healing hypnosis." She believed it could help me. I decided to try it but was never able to contact her to make an appointment. While I was looking online for information about this hypnosis, I ran into a Facebook post by a man named Noam whose profile had the words "Quantum Healing Hypnosis" written across the top. He wrote, "If you, or anyone you know, is going through something, and you could use some guidance or someone to speak to, or just a listening ear and an open heart, I'm available for you or them. Let's talk. Message me with your number, and I'll call you, or email me, and we'll set up a time. No money exchange, let's just connect. And if you're close by, I'll come see you."

I was willing to try anything. I reached out. Noam said we could speak the following week. "Till then, just try and slow (everything) down and pay close attention to your breathing, the sounds and feelings of it," he wrote. "Every time you catch yourself focusing on something else, go back to your breath. Slow down, inside and out. There's nothing you can't handle, the evidence of that is that you're alive. This, too, will pass. It just stings a bit… you've been stung before. The breath keeps you out of the dark spirals. The mind is the breath's adversary."

The following week, we spoke for about an hour, and Noam said a lot of things that made sense. He talked a lot about focusing on my breath and told me the chaos was only in my head. Outside of my head, the world was beautiful. I knew he was speaking the truth, but I couldn't apply this truth to my own life. It wouldn't change what happened.

Two days later, Noam checked in on me, and I told him I still felt lost. We spoke again, in more detail about our previous conversation, and again, it was a good distraction. When I hung up the phone, however, my hopelessness returned. Two more dark weeks passed before Noam messaged me again. "I am trying to hang in there," I wrote back. "It's tough. The darkness and regret looms over me every day. The future is scary. I had it all, and then it was all gone in an instant. It's overwhelming thinking about what I'm going to do."

"You said it, the FUTURE is scary, but the present isn't all that bad," Noam wrote. "If you had it all and now you don't, it obviously wasn't 'all' because you're still here. Maybe there's a different definition to 'all' that life is trying to show you."

I asked him how I could let go of the guilt and forgive myself. "A man who only knows and identifies himself as angry can only get angry. A man who identifies as depressed can only respond as sad," he replied. "You can only be who you are. Your guilt comes from thinking you should've responded as a different person than you really are. You are who you are, until you identify differently, and then you are something else…but it's still who you are. You don't have to forgive yourself, really, because you didn't do anything wrong. You just need to pay more attention to your thinking, which is driving you mad. It's telling you that you should've been different or done things differently. Don't believe it."

I knew Noam was right, but my reality was emptiness. Still, I continued to reach out to him, and he would advise me to stay calm and out of your mind, to take some time to just sit and close my eyes, watch my breath and pay attention to my heartbeat. When the hopelessness became overwhelming and suicidal ideations began, he suggested I should try accepting that there was a cloud over me and that was just the way it was right then. "Only when you accept yourself, and where you are at right now, can you begin to feel better," he said. "If you keep trying to make yourself better without accepting why you are depressed to begin with, you'll be doing this for a very long time."

He suggested I read *The Power of Now: A Guide to Spiritual Enlightenment* by Eckhart Tolle and two books by Don Miguel Ruiz, *The Four Agreements: A Practical Guide to Personal Freedom* and *Voice of Knowledge, and Mastery of Love: A Practical Guide to the Art of Relationship,* like my life depended on it…because it did. I read *The Four Agreements,* but I still felt exhausted, constantly struggling against overwhelming sadness, hopelessness, and loneliness. Noam suggested I find a more physical experience of acceptance, through a method that uses breath as the doorway back to myself. Desperate for anything that could help, I immediately opened the link Noam sent to a YouTube video about a breathing technique called the Wim Hof Method (WHM).

I watched the short video, then replayed it, following along this time, doing a round of deep breathing that made me feel a buzz unlike anything I'd ever felt before, a lightening of the world's weight and a subtle euphoria that grew with every breath cycle. I felt like every cell of my body was awakening and refreshing, like receiving a saline solution drip when you're extremely dehydrated or hungover. I repeated a few rounds and immediately felt better. I knew I had discovered something powerful, and a small wave of hope rolled through me.

In 1995, the year I graduated from high school, Wim Hof's wife, who suffered from schizophrenia and bipolar disorder, had jumped to her death from the eighth floor of a building, devastating Hof and their four children.[63][64] Plunged into the depths of depression, Hof found relief in the powers of cold exposure, which he had discovered as a young man many years earlier. After jumping into the frigid waters at his home in the Netherlands, he found he felt much better. During his soul-searching journey over the next several decades, Hof explored many disciplines and esoteric studies as he pushed himself, exploring his body's potential when faced with nature's raw power. His search culminated in the development of a breathing technique that allowed him to endure extremely cold temperatures, achieving feats previously thought impossible for the human body.

"Over time, we as humans have developed a different attitude towards nature, and we've forgotten about our inner power," Hof states. "This is the ability of our body to adapt to extreme temperatures and survive within our natural environment." The WHM is based on this principle. Hof believes wearing clothes and artificially controlling the temperature in our homes and workplaces greatly reduces our bodies' natural stimulation, causing the mechanisms related to our survival and basic functions to atrophy. "Because these deeper physiological layers are no longer triggered, our bodies are no longer in touch with this inner power," he states. "The inner power is a powerful force that can be reawakened by stimulating these physiological processes through the Wim Hof Method."

Hof put himself to the test to prove his theory time and time again, breaking twenty-six world records in the process. In 2007, he ran a half marathon in Finland, above the polar circle, wearing only shorts. A few months later, he climbed Mount Everest wearing only shorts and boots, but because of a foot injury sustained during the half marathon, he made it only to 7,200 meters, just shy of the summit.[65][66] To test whether his extreme temperature tolerance also worked with heat, Hof ran a full marathon in the Namibian desert in forty-degree Celsius (104 Fahrenheit) temperatures without drinking one drop of water; he lost fourteen pounds.[67]

WHM consists of three pillars: a breathing technique, cold exposure, and mindset. The breathing technique involves several cycles of deep breathing, maximizing lung capacity, and breath retention, in which all breath is expelled from the lungs. As carbon dioxide is expelled, oxygen saturation is at its highest, enabling oxygen to roam freely and reach deeply into the body, including the brain stem, or primitive brain, which seldom receives this much oxygen because most breathing in the modern world is very shallow. This effectively reawakens the limbic system, found in the brain stem, which processes fear, memory, and emotions. Optimizing its functions can lead to long-term emotional regulation and control.

The breath cycles also cause the body to become more alkaline, minimizing the acidity that causes disease to thrive and bringing the body closer to homeostasis. They have also been proven to boost the immune system through the conscious secretion of adrenaline, tapping into the autonomous nervous system. In 2011, Hof was injected with a dead cell-wall component of the *E. coli* bacteria, and used his breathing technique to consciously raise his cortisol and epinephrine levels, suppressing and resetting his immune response to prevent the fever, chills, and headache the endotoxin normally causes. Even more impressive, he trained twelve volunteers in ten days to pass the same test.[68] [69]

Scientists are beginning to unravel the mechanisms behind the WHM miracle. When oxygen availability is low, a state called hypoxia, the body creates erythropoietin (EPO) to increase production of red blood cells, which transport oxygen from the lungs to all body tissues.

(Endurance athletes sometimes use EPO to increase their supply of oxygen-carrying red blood cells.) Within this biological feedback loop is a class of proteins called hypoxia-inducible factors (HIF), which accumulate in cells under hypoxic conditions, then bind to hypoxia-inducible elements (HIE) in thousands of target genes that act as a switch to produce EPO. In other words, HIF regulates oxygen homeostasis. As HIF accumulates in the body, specific genes are turned on to increase EPO, which, in turn, increases the effectiveness of oxygen supply at the cellular level. WHM is a very effective tool for manipulating oxygen levels in the body, thus inducing these biochemical chain reactions. During breath retention, cells sense the oxygen shortage and adapt so they will be fit for future oxygen shortages. The breath cycles also boost white blood cells, increasing the body's ability to defend itself against bacteria, viruses, and disease.[70]

The second pillar of WHM is cold exposure, usually through ice baths. When the body is exposed to freezing temperatures, its sympathetic/parasympathetic nervous systems, also known as fight/flight and rest/digest response, are stimulated. Controlled breathing suppresses the initial sympathetic nervous system response and induces the parasympathetic nervous system (rest/digest), reducing anxiety and stress over time and leading to increased emotional control and an increasing sense of inner peace. Icy temperatures also trigger secretion of many feel-good hormones, such as norepinephrine, causing a euphoric feeling that can last for several hours, and cause vasoconstriction of every vein and artery, strengthening the cardiovascular system and improving circulation. Possibly the most important benefit of cold exposure is that it reduces full-body inflammation, which is why ice therapy is ubiquitous in sports training and rehabilitation. Inflammation can cause "sickness behaviors,'" including physical, cognitive, and behavioral changes,[71] including depression, loss of appetite, sleep disturbance, anhedonia (loss of pleasure), cognitive impairment, and suicidal ideation.[72]

The third pillar of WHM is mindset. Recent research by Dr. Andrew Huberman, neurobiologist and ophthalmologist at Stanford University, shows that mindset affects our physiology. Whether we believe we can do something or not and whether we believe that action is beneficial to us or not affects the physiological outcome of the event. It is literally mind over matter. Knowing we can overcome one of the most evolutionarily feared of the elements—cold—fosters an extreme sense of confidence. Starting every morning with an ice-cold shower, an intense physical sensation, also facilitates deep meditation, which has unlimited benefits as well.

Using fMRI and positron emission tomography (PET), Wayne State University School of Medicine professors Otto Muzik, PhD, and Vaibhav Diwadkar, PhD, have studied how Hof's brain responds during experimentally controlled, whole-body cold exposure and found "compelling brain processes in Wim Hof." Hof's breathing technique made his skin temperature relatively invariant to cold. The researchers observed substantial activation in an area of the upper brainstem called the periaqueductal gray matter, which is believed to control sensory pain through the release of opioids and cannabinoids.[73] The researchers hypothesize that by "generating a stress-induced analgesic response in periaqueductal gray matter, the Wim Hof Method may promote the spontaneous release of opioids and cannabinoids in the brain. This effect has the potential to create a feeling of well-being, mood control, and reduced anxiety." They went on to say this suggests "intriguing possibilities for how his techniques might exert positive effects related to disorders of the immune system and even psychiatry."[74] Diwadkar stated: "The practice of the Wim Hof Method may lead to tonic changes in autonomous brain mechanisms, a speculation that has implications for managing medical conditions ranging from diseases of the immune system to more intriguingly psychiatric conditions such as mood and anxiety disorders."

I experimented daily with this new breathing technique and found it could lift my mood for a good while, but the darkness always returned. It wasn't until I did the breath cycles after eating the mushrooms that I really felt the intense euphoria and massive mind shift it provides. I realized I had only been putting about 50 percent effort into the breathing, but after my mushroom experience, I started giving it my all and incorporating the ice baths.

Feeling the connection between my breath and the present moment brought me out of my head, just like Noam promised. For hours following a WHM breathing session, my mood is elevated, my energy is high, and I have a deep sense of inner peace. Not only does it counteract depression, stress, and anxiety, but reliably alters my state of consciousness, which has powerful, lasting positive mental effects. I am physically, mentally, and emotionally healthier and stronger than I've ever been, and I haven't gotten sick since I started practicing WHM. Even when I'm faced with enormous challenges and difficulties, I can ward off the negative thought patterns I was once locked into. I am much more able to manage my attitude, outlook, resourcefulness, and willpower to work through even the most difficult situations.

Researchers have found that in addition to activating our cannabinoid and opioid systems (the endogenous, natural, vital, non-addictive kind), the WHM also activates dopamine, serotonin, epinephrine, nor-epinephrine, adrenaline, and nor-adrenaline, and even DMT—the same feel-good hormones, biological systems, and receptors that are activated by drugs like cannabis, MDMA, psychedelics, and heroin.[75] WHM sessions boost the immune system, allow us to gain control over our autonomous nervous system, change our brain chemistry, and optimize all of our biological processes. Our minds become fused with and highly aware of our bodies.

Many times during my morning practice, I experience euphoria stronger than any drug I've ever tried. I can make myself feel even better than when I'm skiing, surfing, or rock climbing by simply breathing. I am essentially microdosing on my own endorphins, opioids, cannabinoids, and DMT, becoming healthier and stronger in the process. I can ski the Alps, surf Hawaii, or climb El Capitan, all in the comfort of my own home. It is truly a blessing, and all it takes is air, cold water, and a healthy dose of discipline and willpower.

During my mushroom journey, I practiced the WHM a few times and could actually feel Noam's words: "If breath is life, and you have known breath to be autonomous, this is showing you that you are consciously choosing when to breathe. You become aware of your choice to live life, and every breath becomes a decision. These breathless states can offer you the presence and awareness of being in choice to be breathless. Keep practicing, you will begin to feel calmness that you never knew existed and begin to feel peace. This peace is your true nature, it is always there, you just cloud it with your mind. Out of mind, back into the body. This will change your life."

I had no idea how massively the WHM would change my life, but I knew I was onto something big. Oxygen optimizes brain function, which, in turn, optimizes every function in the body. What synergy occurred when I practiced Wim Hof breathing while on mushrooms? Did it enhance the psilocybin effect? After each breath cycle, I was sent flying out of my head with an intense euphoria engulfing me from head to toe. It seems plausible that if psilocybin has the power to reboot and reset neurological connections in my brain, increasing blood flow to the brain and maximizing oxygen consumption with the breath cycles would enhance those effects and my brain's neuroplasticity, giving this neurological reboot an added boost.

YOGA & MEDITATION

You are not your mind. ~ *Eckhart Tolle*

6 a.m.: Wake up. Make the bed. Go to the bathroom. Roll out the yoga mat. Begin.

My routine for the last three years didn't come easy and is still far from perfect, but the positive effects I felt from it were immediate. When I was still fine tuning my routine, I had to beat my mind to the mat in the morning, asking myself, who is going to be in control today, my ego or me?

Maybe you have experienced waking up feeling troubled, unsure why. You begin your day worried about something you can't quite put your finger on. Usually, it's a distressing dream or nightmare that fades away upon waking, but the physiological stress response, anxiety, lingers. The next thing you know, you're arguing with your spouse and worrying about all the things that might go wrong today. To-do list? Family? My brother Leo, who saved my life by suggesting I take magic mushrooms, is gravely ill, and we don't know why. My mother is entering her elderly years, and her health and well-being weigh heavily on my mind. My family relations are strained at best. Ego still prevails in lifelong family battles. Where will I find the money to publish my book? These things are always on my mind.

I had to train myself to circumvent my brain's need to start worrying as soon as I woke up, keeping the thoughts out while I go to the bathroom and get my yoga mat out immediately. Before I began my yoga training, I would wake up in cold sweats from horrid nightmares about my ex-wife and my previous life, if I was lucky to get any sleep at all. Awake or not, my thoughts were killing me.

When I realized I had been liberated from the torment of ego after my mushroom journey and given a second chance, I put to use the tools I had stumbled across. One of them was yoga. If I begin the day with a yoga session, followed by a Wim Hof breathing session, the dark thoughts keep their distance throughout the day. When I miss a day or don't fully focus on my routine, the darkness starts to invade my mental territory. My routine is like a guard dog keeping the monsters outside the gate.

Confidence in my routine grew over the months as the nightmares subsided and waking thoughts began filling my awareness with beauty, gratitude, and love. By adhering to a strict, non-negotiable, morning routine, I'm able to maintain my daily disposition at ecstatic—and climbing—regardless of the circumstances. I have fallen in love with life again, and yoga has been an integral part of this journey. To love life, we must love ourselves. To love ourselves, we must love our body, and to love our body, we must put it to use. Out of the head, into the body. As the Roman emperor Marcus Aurelius observed, "Nowhere can man find a quieter, or more untroubled retreat, than in his own soul."

As my practice grew over that first year of recovery, it morphed from guard dog to best friend. My sense of inner peace grew, and then it really clicked. It hit me one particularly stressful day at work, when I realized all I had to do was breathe, and everything would be fine. I continued what I was doing, intently focused on my breath, and—just as I had promised myself—everything turned out just fine. I realized this is exactly what I do during yoga: focus on my breath as I contort my body into strange, difficult, and therefore stressful positions. Yoga trains the mind to do this throughout the day through muscle memory. When we focus on the breath, all problems dissipate because our breath lives in the present moment, where problems cannot reside. We can't think about anything else while focusing on the breath—try, and you will see.

Of all the analogies for this concept, the first that

resonated with me was of a kite representing our thoughts, with the string as our breath. An uncontrolled string leads to an uncontrolled kite, but by carefully tending to the string, applying tension to it, reeling it in when necessary, you can remain in control of the kite, in control of your mind. Another is the monkey mind analogy. As we know too well, our thoughts tend to flutter about without aim or direction, usually looking for trouble. If we think of our mind as a monkey, we can give the monkey a job so it stays busy and out of trouble. The monkey's job is simple: to count our breaths. In this way, our attention stays on the breath, not on our countless fears, worries, and concerns.

Worrying rarely, if ever, pays off. As the Stoic philosopher Seneca noted 2,000 years ago, "We are more often frightened than hurt and we suffer more often from imagination than from reality." Our thoughts create our reality. Simple concept, extremely difficult to achieve. It is a journey that humans have been exploring for thousands of years.

Meditation and yoga have been deeply intertwined since at least 5000 BCE in India, the birthplace of both practices, though some sources believe they originated as far back as 8000 BCE. In the sixth century BCE in India, a man named Siddhartha Gautama left his life as a royal prince to seek enlightenment, discovering meditation and philosophy along the way. He soon developed his own methodology, which became known as Buddhism, and spent the next several decades teaching meditation and spiritual awakening to thousands of people in India. Buddhism spread throughout Asia over the next several centuries.[76]

Yoga was developed as a technique to facilitate deep meditation. Ancient yogis figured out that a flexible, limber body carried over to a flexible, limber mind. The word "yoga" is derived from the Sanskrit word *yuji*, which means "yoke" or "union" (of the body and mind). Many of the stone-carved figures of the original yoga postures found in the Indus Valley show people seated in meditative postures with eyes half-closed. The oldest written reference to meditation dates back to 1500 BCE in the Vedas, ancient Hindu scriptures about how to live in accordance with the universal order of the cosmos, written in early Sanskrit but preserved by oral tradition for millennia. Subjects include health, science, economics, astrology, and warfare, among others. The origin of the Vedas, and in turn, yoga, is quite a mystery and a bit controversial; many experts believe they simply appeared with no known source.

The concept of yoga came from the Rig Veda. Included in the Vedas was a separate group of wisdom teachings known as the Upanishads, which include mini stories embedded with yogic teachings. The Upanishads teach that liberation is not only for spiritual gurus or holy men, and by applying these teachings to everyday life, anyone's mind can be liberated. These teachings are the foundation of yoga, Hinduism, and Buddhism, which is why there is some crossover in traditions and similarities in practices. In ancient times, meditation was a practice for religious people and wandering ascetics who sought to transcend the limitations of human consciousness, connect with universal forces personified as deities, and come into union with the transcendental reality called Brahman.

The Hindu tradition of meditation is the oldest meditation tradition on Earth, still in practice today.[77] The modern yoga movement, which heavily emphasizes the physical aspects of postures and breathing exercises, is an adaptation of the Hatha Yoga school, one of the hundreds of variations. Yoga began, however, as a wisdom tradition focused on meditation and spiritual development, a way to achieve harmony between the heart and soul as a necessary step on the path to divine enlightenment. Yoga is to meditation as chemistry is to science, an essential component, originally one and the same.

Swami Vivekananda brought yoga to America in 1893.[78] He believed the world religions were "but various phases of one eternal religion" and that spiritual essence could be transmitted from one person to another. When he addressed his "sisters and brothers of America" at the World Parliament of Religions in Chicago, his first and most influential speech in the United States, the audience burst out in a standing ovation. So began a steady stream of Eastern ideas flowing west. In 1920, Paramahansa Yogananda, sent by his guru Babaji to "spread the message of Kriya yoga to the West," addressed a conference of religious liberals in Boston as the yoga movement grew in America. A few years later, the United States immigration service imposed a quota on Indian immigration, forcing Westerners to travel to the East to seek yogic teachings and slowing down the wave of yoga that had hit the United States. Forty-one years later, in 1965, the immigration law was revised to remove the quota, sparking a new wave of Eastern teachers.[79]

Yoga was established on the West Coast in the mid-1950s when two students of Yogananda, Walt and Magana Baptiste, started a studio in San Francisco.[80] The family yoga dynasty continues today with their children, Baron and Sherri. Meditation and yoga then exploded across America in the early 1960s. In 1966, B.K.S. Iyengar's *Light on Yoga*, still considered the bible of asana practice, was published in the United States.[81] Ram Dass, a former Harvard professor who was expelled because of his involvement with the Harvard Psilocybin Project, became another influential figure for the yoga movement in the United States when he published *Be Here Now* in 1971.[82] By the early 1970s, yoga studios were popping up all across the country.

In 1970, at the Menninger Foundation in Topeka, Kansas, Yogi Swami Rama astonished researchers when he demonstrated he could control his autonomic nervous system, including his heartbeat, blood pressure, and body temperature, by means of meditation.[83] He altered his heartbeat up to 300 beats per minute for 16 seconds while sitting motionless and then, within a few minutes, completely stopped his heart from pumping blood for a few seconds. He also altered the skin temperature on adjacent sides of his hand by consciously dilating and contracting his blood vessels with his mind; produced alpha, delta, theta, and gamma brain waves on demand; and remained fully conscious of his environment while his brain was in deep sleep.

Swami Rama's astonishing meditation demonstrations launched a growing body of research confirming the health benefits of yoga and meditation. Multiple studies have shown that yoga can reduce secretion of cortisol, our primary stress hormone, reducing stress and anxiety. In 2005, a German study of twenty-four women who perceived themselves as emotionally distressed found they had significantly lower levels of cortisol and reported lower levels of stress, anxiety, fatigue, and depression after a three-month yoga program.[84] Two years later, an Australian study of 131 people had similar results, showing that ten weeks of yoga reduced stress and anxiety in the participants.[85] Yoga practice lowered anxiety in women diagnosed with anxiety disorders in an Iranian study[86] and reduced PTSD symptoms in women in a 2014 study at the Trauma Center at Justice Resource Institute in Brookline, Maryland.[87]

Because cortisol levels influence serotonin, the neurotransmitter often associated with depression, yoga has shown remarkable potential in battling depression. In a 2006 study in India, participants in an alcohol addiction program who practiced Sudarshan Kriya, which focuses on rhythmic breathing, had lower levels of cortisol and fewer symptoms of depression.[88] Yoga has also shown potential to reduce inflammation, which can be an underlying cause of depression and many illnesses. In 2014, a small study at UCLA showed that 12 weeks of yoga reduced inflammation in breast cancer survivors suffering from chronic fatigue.[89]

It's also proving beneficial against high blood pressure and heart disease. An English study found that participants over 40 years of age who practiced yoga for five years had lower blood pressure and pulse rate than those who didn't.[90] In a 2004 study at the Yoga Institute in Santacruz, Mumbai, India, 113 patients with heart disease who completed one year of yoga training combined with dietary modifications and stress management saw a 23 percent decrease in total cholesterol and a 26 percent reduction in LDL cholesterol. Heart disease stopped progressing in 47 percent of the patients.[91] Other studies have found that yoga can improve sleep quality and duration, and reduced the need for sleep medications[92] and reduce migraine intensity, frequency, and pain.[93]

As these scientific experiments demonstrate, yoga and meditation are extremely effective tools in combating many physical and mental ailments, as well as optimizing every aspect of our health. In the midst of deep meditation, the calmness we feel is reality. It is here where we connect to our inner power and the vast expanse of the universe. Yogis have professed for millennia that the breath is the gateway to the soul, the place where problems dissipate. Stillness provides the correct lens from which to peer out at the universe, clear of the noise, chatter, and chaos that clutters our mind and distorts our reality. Yoga is a powerful tool to ground us in the present moment. As Noam told me early in our conversations, "The chaos is only in your head. Outside, the world is calm and beautiful." Or as Ram Dass put it, "The quieter you become, the more you can hear."

I believe the world's problems are simply societal manifestations of the problem we struggle with as individuals: the battle with our ego. The chaos that occurs in the mind of the individual is re-multiplied by nearly 8 billion; when ego wins and multiplies, it gives rise to cultural, national, and societal ego, driven by fear and resentment, and this gives rise to war and greed.

There is hope. In Havana, Cuba, on June 23, 2016, Sri Sri Ravi Shankar, founder of The Art of Living, brokered a unilateral ceasefire between the Colombian government and the Revolutionary Armed Forces of Colombia (FARC), which had been locked in a fifty-year war with the Colombian government that had claimed more than 220,000 lives, most of them civilians, and displaced more than 5 million people. During meetings between Colombian President Juan Manuel Santos and the FARC peace delegation led by Ivan Marquez, Shankar insisted that both parties "adopt the Gandhian principle of non-violence and cultivate the art of meditation and breathing." The Republic of Colombia later awarded Shankar with the highest civilian award, the Simón Bolivar Order, for his peace work, and The Art of Living began teaching stress relief and meditation to FARC members in an effort to "help create peace on the individual level." Ivan Marquez, FARC's chief negotiator, stated, "With the help of Sri Sri, we have placed our spirit to achieve reconciliation and coexistence of a big and benevolent country whose destiny cannot be that of the war. ... The teachings of The Art of Living are essential to achieve a stable and long-lasting peace. We hope that the peace of Colombia serves as a source of inspiration for the world."[94]

To win the battle against humanity's dark side, we must first win the battle within ourselves. It all starts with the individual, right here, right now, in the present moment. The highest form of human intelligence is the ability to observe ourselves without judgment.

~Namaste

STOIC PHILOSOPHY

You could leave life right now. Let that determine what you do, and say, and think.
~ Marcus Aurelius

I wasn't sure what the aftermath of my psychedelic journey would bring. I was aware of recent success in treating depression with psychedelics, but I couldn't imagine what it would feel like to be happy again. The day after my first mushroom journey, I woke up feeling refreshingly positive, but I went about the day feeling a bit apprehensive, waiting for the darkness to return. The day came and went with no sign of it—in fact, it was a great day—and the next day was the same. The third day, Christmas Day, I woke up so enthusiastic that I had lived two days free of depression that I decided to start reading entrepreneur articles again. I'd stopped reading them when my life fell apart and all my motivation seeped away. As I began to see light at the end of the tunnel, I figured I would have to start somewhere to create a new life.

The first article I came across was about three powerful ideas that can change your life. One of them was to carry a coin that has the Latin phrase *memento mori* ("remember we must die") along with an interpretation of French painter Philippe de Champaigne's seventeenth-century painting, "Still Life with a Skull," depicting the only three things that are real: a tulip, representing life; a skull, representing death; and an hourglass, representing time. The other side of the coin says, "You could leave life right now," a shortened line from Roman emperor and Stoic philosopher Marcus Aurelius. The full quote reads, "You could leave right now. Let that determine what you do and say and think." The coin is meant to be a tangible reminder to create priority and urgency in our lives and to treat our time in this life as a gift. I had just gone through my father's passing, and this struck me hard. I decided to order the coin and look into this Stoicism thing. I had no idea how much of an influence Stoicism would have on me and how much this little coin would change my life.

I've never been religious, though my parents tried hard to convert me. My mom and I joke now about how she would bribe me with her car to get me to go to church. I sat through the preaching a few times because I was a teenager and I needed a car, but her attempts to convert me were futile. So, when I came across Stoic philosophy and learned it was secular, not dependent on faith but rather on a logical system of ethics—more of an actionable operating system, a school for how to live life, which is sorely missing in our education system today—I was enthralled. Stoicism and I were meant to be.

Even more amazing, evidence now shows that ancient Stoics used psychedelics at Eleusis, which most likely was the source of many of their insights. In fact, this new evidence points to the possibility that all of Western philosophy, including democracy itself, was conceived during the elite's ergot-fueled psychedelic rituals at Eleusis. I find this striking because I accidentally stumbled across Stoic philosophy a few days after my mushroom journey, and the writings made so much sense. They are the kinds of thoughts I naturally think during psychedelic experiences, and I had a personal theory that the creators of Stoic philosophy had to be taking psychedelics to think these thoughts. Sure enough, they were! The combination of psychedelics and Stoic philosophy is so powerful because it is the exact modality that some of the greatest thinkers in history have used to develop modern society.

Stoic philosophy, founded by Zeno of Citium (current-day Cyprus) in Athens in the early third century BCE, is heavily influenced by the teachings of Socrates and Plato. It was born in a time of uncertainty, during a transition of the gods when humans "stood alone" in the universe and had to answer the big questions themselves. What is life? How should it be lived? What is important? What is ethical? Stoicism takes its name from the place where Zeno often lectured, the Stoa Poikile, meaning "painted colonnade," in Athens, Greece.[95] [96] Zeno was a wealthy merchant from a prominent family with a fleet of ships until a storm sank them all. He ended up in Athens with nothing in his pockets. Before starting his school of Stoicism, he studied at Plato's academy in Athens for ten years. His lost treatise, *Pythagorean Teachings*, held theories of the universe similar to those of Pythagoras, who coined the term *kosmos*, which means "a beautiful order." (This is the origin of the word cosmetic.) Saying the universe is beautiful, therefore, is a factual statement. The Greeks believed the universe was beautiful because of *harmonia*, modern-day harmony, which originally meant "fitting together."

With the death of Aristotle in 322 BCE and Alexander the Great in 323 BCE, Athens' dominance began its decline and its cultural prominence passed primarily to Rome. Though the specific timeline is still under debate, Stoicism rose up roughly between the age of Cicero (106-43 BCE) and Marcus Aurelius (121-180 AD) during the transition from polytheism to Christianity in the fourth century.[97] During those years, Stoicism flourished as a philosophy of personal ethics dictated by its system of logic and views on the natural world. The dissolution of the gods as the guiding light forced humans to turn inwards to search for answers, which came in the form of logic, reason, and virtue. Though Aurelius wasn't technically a philosopher, he used Stoicism as a framework for dealing with the stresses of daily life as emperor. *Meditations*, a collection of journals he kept throughout his twenty-year reign, may be the most authentic work of philosophy ever created, as his notes were not meant for anyone else to read. Aurelius's notes to himself on how to be a better person, emperor, husband, and family man essentially document his journey of self-improvement.

The four virtues of Stoic philosophy, derived from the teachings of Plato, are wisdom, courage, justice, and temperance. According to Stoicism, the path to happiness is found in accepting the present moment as it is and not allowing ourselves to be driven by uncontrolled emotions—controlled by the desire for pleasure or fear of pain—by using our minds to understand the universe and adhere to and actively contribute to nature's plan. The Stoics called this *eudaimonia*, which directly translates to "happiness," though equanimity is a better description.[98] They believed happiness depends on controlling our emotions, being even-keeled, and not swaying too much in either direction and that humans could free themselves of suffering through *apatheia*, translated as "without passion." Cleanthes of Assos (330 BCE - 230 BCE) said that "the wicked man is like a dog tied to a cart and compelled to go wherever it goes," meaning our emotions dragging us anywhere they want is the source of our suffering. The word "stoic" has come to mean "unemotional" in today's world, but the Stoics did not seek to simply extinguish emotions. Rather, they trained themselves to react accordingly to them by a system of logic and reflection, to rise above the emotional turmoil caused by our own thinking.

The Stoics believed virtue is the only good and could be achieved by clearly identifying what is in our control and what is not, then solely focusing and acting on the former. With training, we can learn to view all life events as external and outside of our control, understanding that only our judgment of them is within our control. This is known as the "dichotomy of control." As Epictetus said 2,000 years ago, "We suffer not from events in our lives, but from our judgment about them." Epictetus believed molding our will and conforming our desires to suit the natural world would allow us to be "sick and yet happy, in peril and yet happy, dying and yet happy, in exile and happy, in disgrace and happy."[99]

Believing that everything was rooted in nature, which is rational, the Stoics therefore saw it as imperative to understand the rules of the natural order. When faced with an ethical dilemma, turning to nature and observing its rules and systems was the appropriate methodology. They believed all suffering could be prevented by examining our judgments and behavior and identifying where they diverge from the natural order. One example is the Stoics' view of slavery. Though Seneca owned slaves, his opinion of slavery was revolutionary for the time. He believed even slaves were "equals of other men, because all men alike are products of nature" and admonished, "Kindly remember that he whom you call your slave sprang from the same stock, is smiled upon by the same skies, and on equal terms with yourself, breathes, lives, and dies."[100]

Aurelius believed that "to understand our own nature, we must understand the nature of the world from which we emerged. Without an understanding of the nature of the universe, a man cannot know where he is. Without an understanding of its purpose, he cannot know what he is or what the universe itself is. Either of these discoveries be hidden from him, he will not be able so much as to give a reason for his own existence." This, Aurelius believed, is why the study of the cosmos is so important. "Always think of the universe as one living organism with a single substance, and a single soul, and observe how all things are submitted to the single perceptivity of this one whole. All are moved by its single impulse, and all play their part in the causation of every event that happens. In an organism, all the individual parts exist not to go off in their own direction, but to work for the benefit of the whole. We have come into being to work together like feet, hands, eyelids, or the two rows of teeth in our upper and lower jaws. To work against one another is, therefore, contrary to nature."

In what the Stoics called *cosmopolis,* Aurelius explained,

"all things are interwoven with one another; a sacred bond unites them; there is scarcely one thing that is isolated from one another. Everything is coordinated, everything works together in giving form to the one universe." Seneca believed "the universe that you see containing the human and the divine is a unity. We are limbs of a mighty body. Nature brought us to birth as kin, since it generated us all from the same materials, and for the same purposes, endowing us with affection for one another and making us companionable. Let us hold all things in common, as we are born for the common good. Our companionship is just like a stone arch, which would collapse without the stones' mutual support to hold it up." The Stoics' emphasis on the universal fellowship of humanity provided the foundation for the early Christian idea of "the brotherhood of humanity" and "love thy neighbor." There are, in fact, many parallels between Stoicism and Christianity.

The beauty of this philosophy is that we can confirm this interconnectedness by observing nature rather than taking it on faith. Observing the fractal geometry in nature reveals patterns that scale in everything. Everything in the universe develops physically in accordance with the geometry of nature. Smaller parts fit geometrically, as optimally as possible, to function as part of the greater whole. Plato said the "world soul" is the intelligent and harmonious principle of proportion that exists at the heart of nature, or cosmic pattern, which allows nature's living forms to unfold in the most elegant way. In *Timaeus*, Plato wrote that the universe is "one whole of wholes" and a "single living creature that contains all living creatures within it." Aurelius said, "We are not merely 'parts' of the whole, but 'limbs' of the universe. If we think of ourselves only as parts, we act only out of 'bare duty,' and not out of 'love from the heart of mankind.'"

The Stoics believed we were born to be ethical because we are parts of humanity, united by kinship and universal reason, like the parts of an organism, designed to serve or benefit the whole. This is why a major component of Stoic philosophy is the practice of relatedness. Knowing we are "limbs" and not simply independent agents with individual agendas not only fosters ethical behavior but also helps reduce feelings of isolation, which fuel loneliness and depression. This perspective could be very useful in today's modern world with its ever-increasing rates of depression and an environmental crisis, exacerbated by individualistic thinking, which threatens our very existence.

Humans must learn to coexist in accordance and in unison with each other and with the natural world, according to the laws of nature—just as a school of fish moves in unison to look like a larger animal to predators or a flock of birds flies together because it is aerodynamically advantageous to work together rather than fly solo. Those who work together, with nature, flourish. Those who don't, perish.

Stoicism has influenced every corner of history and culture. The United States came to be because the founding fathers were heavily influenced by Stoic philosophy.[101] Thomas Jefferson kept a copy of Seneca on his night stand, and George Washington staged a reproduction of a play about Cato to inspire the troops at Valley Forge.

The list of modern-day Stoics includes Bill Clinton, James Mattis, Arnold Schwarzenegger, Joe Madden, Tom Brady, Ben Roethlisberger, Ralph Waldo Emerson, JK Rowling, Robert Greene, and Neil Strauss.[102] Alex Hannold's free solo of El Capitan in Yosemite required a complete control of fear that struck me as extremely Stoic. Failure meant certain death, and he had to not only accept, but embrace, that possible outcome. James Stockdale, who was shot down in Vietnam and taken prisoner by the

North Vietnamese, spent seven years in captivity subjected to torture, isolation, and unimaginable terror. He survived because he never lost control of what no one could take from him: his mind. "I never lost faith in the end of the story," he said. "I never doubted not only that I would get out, but also that I would prevail in the end and turn the experience into the defining event of my life, which, in retrospect, I would not trade."[103]

Tim Ferriss, author of *The Four-Hour Workweek*—the book that inspired me to change my life—gave a Ted Talk in which he reveals that, at one point in his life, he had decided to kill himself. He had suffered from bipolar depression and had had at least fifty depressive episodes. "I was sitting in the back of my used minivan in a campus parking lot when I decided I was going to commit suicide," Ferris said. "I went from deciding to full- blown planning very quickly. And I came close to the edge of the precipice. It's the closest I've ever come."

Thanks to a few lucky coincidences, Ferris did not pull the trigger. "After the fact, the thing that scared me the most was the element of chance. So, I became very methodical about testing different ways that I could manage my ups and downs. And the tool I've found which has proven to be the most reliable safety net for emotional free-fall is actually the same tool that has helped me to make my best business decisions, but that is secondary. And it is… Stoicism."

He describes Stoicism as an "operating system for thriving in high-stress environments, for making better decisions." By training yourself to "separate what you can control from what you cannot control, and then doing exercises to focus exclusively on the former," we can "decrease emotional reactivity, which can be a superpower. Let's say you're a quarterback. You miss a pass. You get furious with yourself. That could cost you a game. If you're a CEO, and you fly off the handle at a very valued employee because of a minor infraction, that could cost you the employee. If you're a college student who, say, is in a downward spiral, and you feel helpless and hopeless, unabated, that could cost you your life. So, the stakes are very, very high."

Ferris stumbled across Stoicism after buying a book on simplicity, trying to find ways to cope with his high-stress, fourteen-hour workdays. The first quote that made a big difference in his life was by Seneca: "We suffer more often in imagination than in reality." This led him to Seneca's *Letters from a Stoic*, which led him to the practice that changed his life, *premeditatio malorum*, which means the "premeditation of evils." Ferris describes the practice as "visualizing the worst-case scenarios in detail that you fear, preventing you from taking action, so that you can take action to overcome that paralysis."

Out of this practice, Ferris developed what he calls "fear setting," recalibrating your fears as close to reality as possible, which he credits for helping him decide to step away from his business and take his first vacation in four years to London, which turned into a year-and-a-half trip around the world, which became the basis for his first book and bestseller, *The Four-Hour Workweek*.[104] Facing and dealing with his fears instead of being consumed by them dramatically changed Tim's life, and as a result, the lives of hundreds, maybe thousands of people. All these people have overcome incredible odds to achieve what they have accomplished. It takes an enormous amount of discipline to fill a Stoic's shoes, but it does indeed become a superpower.

Still, we must never forget the warriors who created Stoicism, who overcame obstacles we can't even fathom in today's world, such as the poor father who had to dine with Roman emperor Caligula after the emperor had had his son executed. The man had pleaded for his son's release, but his pleas had the opposite effect. Caligula had his son executed the very same day, then invited the father to dinner so he could watch him suffer, a royal power play.

The father did not break; he would not allow Caligula to enjoy his suffering. Seneca wrote that he drank the wine offered to him "as though he were drinking his son's blood." He "drank to an extent which would have been hardly decent on a child's birthday; he shed no tear the while; he did not permit his grief to betray itself by the slightest sign; he dined just as though his entreaties had gained his son's life."[105]

We would do well to remember these stories next time we are angry at someone for being rude, feel frustrated because our cars aren't getting us somewhere as fast as we would like, anxious that we may be tight on cash this month, sad that our vacation plans fell through, or even if we have health issues. If these people could overcome such enormous obstacles, we can overcome anything in today's world.

I started studying Stoicism so I could learn how to take control of my mind and emotions by focusing on the present moment, which I achieve by intently focusing on my breath. Instead of being a "dog tied to a cart," I had to learn to happily go wherever the cart takes me. The human experience is a very delicate dance between the present moment, the future, and history, intrinsically tied together and all happening quite literally at the same time. Our reactions to the present moment determine the flow of the dance.

The truth is, we don't actually make anything happen; we react to things already happening around us. If we don't actively lead this dance, our uncontrolled emotions will, and emotions have had their dancing shoes on for millennia. Let's just say they are better dancers. In the words of Aurelius, "The art of living is more like wrestling than dancing, in so far as it stands ready against the accidental and the unforeseen and is not apt to fall."

To lead this dance requires acute awareness and

acceptance of the present moment and a cultivated control of our mind, which fuels our emotions, which determine our reactions. Our untrained emotions are usually in the driver's seat, and we are playing backseat driver with them to no avail. Before we know it, we have been driven to the same ditch we seem incapable of escaping—depression, anxiety, stress, worry—and our lives have fallen apart again. We must learn to take the wheel, silence our emotions, throw them in the trunk, and avoid the ditch.

I also fell in love with Stoicism because of its practicality; Stoic tenets are very specific, concise, highly actionable, and meant to be practiced daily. Another of my favorite Aurelius quotes is, "When you arise in the morning, think of what a precious privilege it is to be alive—to breathe, to think, to enjoy, to love." After several weeks of reading this quote, my gratitude for life skyrocketed and gratitude became the baseline of my existence. It's incredible how malleable the mind is; we truly can train it to think anything we want, and these thoughts turn into reality.

The Stoics believed that only through continual introspection and self-review could we improve in any area of our lives. Seneca said about his journaling practice, "I will keep a constant watch over myself and—most usefully— will put each day up for review."[106] I adopted this practice using a phone app called "The 5 Minute Journal" that gives me a few prompts every morning:

> I am grateful for...
> What will I do to make today great?
> Write down a daily affirmation.

And then before bed, I put the day up for review:

> What amazing things happened today?
> How could I have made today even better?

I immediately began noticing dramatic changes in my thought patterns when I started doing this. Where I had previously been stuck in incessant rumination, I was now thinking positively, grounded in the present moment, and generally excited about life. Journaling was retraining my mind to look for positivity, foster gratitude, and create a sense of responsibility for my actions by continually monitoring myself and constantly looking for areas of improvement. My gratitude for life grew quickly, as did my optimism and general mood.

Along with journaling every day, I made a list of Stoic quotes to serve as a life manual when things get rough, sort of like Epictetus' *Enchiridion*. I would not be caught off guard again. I found the Stoics had countless quotes for every situation life throws at us. As Aurelius' quotes began piling up in my phone, I decided to study him. Noam had told me, "You don't have to recreate the wheel here. There's no better way to spend your time than to read from the masters who have already transformed their life; they were at their ultimate lows and their end with life. They decided to make a change; now they share their wisdom with you."

Over the next several weeks, as I developed a "bulletproof routine" for my mornings, I compiled a list of Stoic quotes to read first thing, to calibrate myself with reality and start the day in the most optimal mind frame. Perhaps the most important of these is the words of Aurelius on the coin I carry in my pocket: *You could leave life right now, let that determine what you do and say and think.*

My father's passing was a deep reminder that we are all going to go at some point; we just have no idea when. It is futile and counterproductive to fear this inevitability. The only choice we have is to make every second count so when we reach that day, we will be happy we didn't waste our life. I believe this defines success. Time is our most valuable resource; everything else is renewable. When you live life by this tenet, you train yourself to be more present and to foster gratitude. Life starts working with you in the most magical ways. Seneca spoke of this idea plenty: "You are living as if destined to live forever; your own frailty never occurs to you; you don't notice how much time has already passed, but squander it as though you had a full and overflowing supply—though all the while that very day which you are devoting to somebody or something may be your last. You act like mortals in all that you fear, and like immortals in all that you desire. ... How late it is to begin really to live, just when life must end! How stupid to forget our mortality and put off sensible plans to our fiftieth and sixtieth years, aiming to begin life from a point at which few have arrived!"

The other coin I carry in my pocket has a Latin phrase popularized by German Stoic philosopher Friedrich Nietzsche: *amor fati* ("love your fate"). Nietzsche believed the formula for human greatness was "not merely to bear what is necessary, but love it." On the front of the coin is a flame, representing Aurelius' words: 'Our inward power, when it obeys nature, reacts to events by accommodating itself to what it faces, to what is possible. It needs no specific material. It pursues its own aims as circumstances allow; it turns obstacles into fuel. As a fire overwhelms what would have quenched a lamp, what's thrown on top of the conflagration is absorbed, consumed by it, and makes it burn still higher." Bestselling author Robert Greene has described the power of *amor fati* as being "so immense that it's almost hard to fathom."

Carrying these coins in my pocket reminds me that all distress is caused by my desire for things to be different. We cannot change the world around us in the present moment; we can only accept it and conform to it. Any notion otherwise is delusion. If we can view life as an enormous string of events all tied together, then the story begins to make sense. We cannot, however, connect the dots looking forward, only looking backwards. We have to trust. If we can believe that the present situation is inherent to our existence, and if we can love our existence, then logically, we must love everything that happens to us, no matter how unbearable it may seem at the time. When we reach this state, there is nothing that can upset or harm us. We are unbreakable when we "love our fate."

Seneca said that "health is the soul that animates all the enjoyments of life, which fade and are tasteless without it." Knowing one day even my good health will decline motivates me to cherish all that I have right now in this moment. This also serves as a preventative measure for minimizing future regret and guilt for not having enjoyed my health when I had it, rendering regret obsolete. When we lose loved ones, it is not the loss that troubles us so much as the guilt we feel that we did not enjoy them while we could have. By doing everything we can now to be present for those around us, we reduce future guilt, knowing we did our best. To live a grateful life in the present moment is to truly live.

Even when I face setbacks, adversity, and misfortunes—and I have plenty, just like anyone else—I get to choose whether they are misfortunes or fortunes. Language and terminology are everything. I get to choose whether to accept adversity and react as positively as I can or fight the present moment and develop a cynical view of life. I get to decide to have a great day, every day, no matter the circumstances. I can achieve this only through relentless practice and training. When adversity inevitably does strike, I borrow from Aurelius' wisdom: 'It's unfortunate this has happened. No, it's fortunate that this has happened to me and I remain unharmed by it, not frightened of the future or shattered by the present. It could've happened to anyone, but not anyone would have remained unharmed....Our actions may be impeded...but there can be no impeding our intentions or dispositions. Because we can accommodate and adapt. The mind adapts and converts to its own purposes the obstacle to our acting."

As I adopted Stoicism, I couldn't help but notice its many similarities to my father's perspective of life. My dad had embarked on a strikingly similar journey to mine to overcome severe depression when I was very young, practicing breathing techniques, cold exposure, and immersing himself in nature. He was, in fact, practicing these techniques during the same years Wim Hof was developing them.

Looking into my dad's history, it struck me that he had been teaching us Stoic lessons his whole life by always wearing a smile, no matter what, aside from those few years when depression sank him. His smile was non-negotiable after his recovery. In our garage in Oceanside, my dad had a poster on the wall with the quote, "Happiness is not having what you want, but wanting what you have." This poster followed us everywhere we lived. It resonated with me back then, and now I understand why. It echoes Seneca's words: "Let us train our minds to desire what the situation demands."

I feel like I'm embodying my dad's spirit, carrying on his life lessons and virtues, as if it were all part of his plan. I was oblivious to his lessons until I needed his strengths, resilience, and virtues to fall in my lap through complete strangers like Noam and a sequence of events I cannot attribute to anything other than the beautiful choreography and synchronicity of the universe. Stoicism has taught me how to flip the script on the events of 2017. It has taught me to navigate life with a smile no matter the situation, fulfilling what I now believe to be my mission in life: to carry forth my dad's lessons, his way of being, his love and lust for life, and to spread his valuable wisdom.

EL HOMBRE FELIZ

*Happiness is not having what you want,
it's wanting what you have.*
~ *Leopoldo Urias*

My father was born on November 15, 1927, in the agricultural village of Revolcaderos, just outside of Culiacan in the mountains of Sinaloa. In letters we have uncovered after his passing, he spoke very fondly of his ranch, his parents, and his family. He truly loved the mountainous landscape and enjoyed his youth despite the overwhelming adversities he encountered. At the age of sixteen, with only a first-grade education, he left the ranch, barefoot, with a *petate (*a floor mat made of straw that rolls up to carry a blanket, customary for a nomadic lifestyle in Mexico in those days) and a *morral* (a sack made for carrying clothes and belongings), to seek a new life. He never liked shoes; he wore them only for work and social events for the rest of his life.

His ancestors, my ancestors, are the Tarahumara Indians, well known for their accomplishments in long-distance running. The Tarahumara frustrated European competitors because they not only won marathons barefoot or wearing homemade *huaraches* (sandals), they did so while taking smoke breaks along the way. Long-distance running literally runs in our blood; "Tarahumara" means "the light-footed one." My brother, sister, nieces, nephews, and I all became top runners in high school. My nephew helped set the 4-by-1,600-meter relay record at Trabuco Hills High School in California, and my sister held the cross- country record at Hueneme High School in Oxnard, California, for many years. I became the top cross- country runner at my high school during my junior year. My dad loved running so much that he embarrassed me by going to cross-country practice with me every day during my first two years of high school—a teenager's worst nightmare. I didn't realize at the time what a blessing that was.

He made his way from the ranch, on the border of Sinaloa and Chihuahua, to Culiacan, then on to Cuidad Obregon, Sonora, where he spent the next several years. Cuidad Obregon was littered with drugs and violence, which formed my dad's aversion to drugs, especially marijuana. One day he stumbled across some kids smoking a joint. They insisted my dad take a puff, but he refused, and the bullies beat him up. He decided to learn to defend himself and began training with local boxers, becoming skilled and winning many competitions. Several months later, he came across the kids that had beat him up, but this time, they were well aware of my dad's boxing accomplishments and attempted to run. My dad told them not to run. Instead of getting revenge, he thanked them for the painful beating that was the reason he learned to box. They apologized for the previous confrontation and developed a mutual respect for my father.

In hindsight, this was the first example of Stoicism I had ever heard. As Seneca put it, "How much better to heal than seek revenge from injury. Vengeance wastes a lot of time and exposes you to many more injuries than the first that sparked it. Anger always outlasts hurt. Best to take the opposite course. Would anyone think it normal to return a kick to a mule or a bite to a dog?" Who knows when my dad's philosophy started resembling Stoic tenets, but it's a theme that became intrinsic to his personality. He told my siblings and me this story many times when we were growing up in his effort to keep us away from drugs, but we never quite believed him. Violent potheads? After researching the history of Mexico in those days, however, it makes sense.

Papi began working with heavy machines and driving

tractors, and his company moved him to Mexicali, where he met Rosario Aguiar, a beautiful young lady who had just moved to Mexicali to work as a secretary in the presidential palace—my mother. (It is believed one of my mother's great, great ancestors was on one of Hernán Cortés' ships during that fateful 1519 expedition to Yucatan.) After they were married, my parents moved to Tijuana, where my dad found work driving a taxi and made extra money in boxing competitions. In 1962, my dad crossed the border and found work picking fruit in Oxnard, California, driving back to Tijuana on weekends to be with his family. He was offered other opportunities driving cement trucks and working as a crane operator, so he moved the whole family to Oxnard. My dad was a *campesino*, a farmer, and he began writing political and social opinion pieces in a local newspaper, *El Campesino,* shortly after arriving in Oxnard. One was about the dangers of marijuana to society. Though my dad's persistent warnings about the dangers of drugs seemed normal for any parent, I now understand his motivations. He never drank a drop of alcohol or touched any drugs.

In my dad's world, drugs meant violence, and violence was a part of life at the ranch. Perhaps that explains the gun we found in his belongings, which he called *la cariñosa* ("the affectionate one"). During a visit with my grandparents at the ranch after my family had settled in Oxnard and a few weeks before I was born, my dad left the car at a gas station because the road to the ranch was rough. When he returned several days later, the military had taken possession of the car and accused him of having drugs in it, a preposterous claim that my dad laughed at. The military and police in Mexico are notorious for planting drugs on unassuming tourists and locals for extortion. Rather than escalate the situation, he returned to Culiacan by bus and a few days later returned with his niece, a local, to vouch for him and reclaim the car.

On the way, two armed men forced my dad out of his

niece's car and started harassing him, asking him why he was stirring up trouble. According to his niece, who got out of the car and hid, the altercation escalated quickly and the men started shooting at my dad. He sprinted back and forth, jumping in the air, dodging the bullets—"like a ninja," is how she described it—and then rushed the men and disarmed the first, binding his hands with his shirt and knocking him out with a large rock to the head before disarming the second man. In a matter of minutes, my dad neutralized the situation and summoned the attention of the local police, who apprehended the men. The whole situation was messy, and because my dad was familiar with Mexico's judicial system, he decided to cut his losses, ensure his niece's safety, and return home to the United States, where he kept the ordeal a secret. He never told us about the violence surrounding the ranch and his family. I believe he wanted to shelter us from the realities of Mexico and the struggles our extended family had to endure. This was his gift to us.

My dad never returned to the ranch after these encounters, which must have broken his heart. He always spoke highly of his family, his parents, and his ranch. In one letter we discovered, he wrote that if he'd known he would never see his mother and father again, he would have returned to the ranch and stayed with them for the rest of their lives. He loved, admired, and missed his family. During his last days, he spoke of wanting to visit the ranch and having dreams of "home." He's not the only dying person to have such dreams; there are thousands of anecdotal reports of the dying having dreams of their dead relatives.[107] Perhaps this is a natural part of the dying process, a way for the mind to comfort itself on its way out. Or are the dead truly waiting for us? Does activation of DMT during the dying process trigger these dreams? Only future research will tell, but when Dad spoke of his ranch, a sense of peace surrounded him. I think he finally visited his longed-for home and family, if only in his mind.

Throughout his ninety years, my dad faced countless life-changing adversities and persevered every time. His resilience was tested time and time again. The second event that shook his world was on a rainy day in 1967. My mom recalls telling him that he shouldn't go to work that day because of the dangerous road conditions, but he was a stubborn, proud man. (My family knows all too well the many times he let his *huevos* (balls) weigh in on his decisions, the hallmark of a *macho Mexicano*.) On the way to work, as he rounded a tight corner over a steep cliff, an oncoming car came too close, forcing him to steer out of the way to avoid a head-on collision. The truck lost its traction, fell over the ravine, and rolled hundreds of feet down the steep cliff to the bottom, almost costing my dad his life again. In what looked like an accident straight out of a movie, he was able to crawl out of the wreckage and seek help, but he suffered a severely broken back and multiple internal injuries. This event changed my family's life and my dad's core beliefs about health and medicine forever.

After several doctors failed to relieve his pain, Dad picked up a book called *Medicina Natural al Alcance de Todos* (*Medicine Within Everyone's Reach*) about natural remedies for pain and ailments with a heavy focus on thermoregulation of the body. He began experimenting with cold water and breathing techniques and found relief in the cold, just as Wim Hof did. He spent a lot of time outdoors in the sun, claiming it had healing properties. After doctors told him he would probably only have a few years to live because of the damage to his internal organs, my dad was able to heal his back over time, relieve all pain associated with it, and became healthier and stronger than he had ever been. He stopped eating processed foods and devoted his life to health, developing many practices that we all thought were crazy—until now, when I find myself doing similar practices and seeing similar results. The coincidental similarities in healing paths my dad, Hof, and I found continue to boggle my mind. It's as if my dad intuitively knew the connection between the sun, serotonin production, gut health, cold exposure, breath work, and even "grounding," as he loved being barefoot, before modern science discovered these ideas.

The accident rendered my dad disabled and unable to keep up with the mortgage on the home he had just purchased. My family ended up homeless, living for a month in our truck. He applied for financial and medical aid, somehow managed to feed the family, and after jumping through several hoops, received enough help to get my family off the streets and back into a rented home. His resilience, perseverance, and dedication to his family's welfare were something to be marveled at. Against all odds, my family survived this period of unemployment, my siblings continued attending school, and a few years later I was born in the small town of Port Hueneme. We moved shortly after my birth to Imperial Beach in San Diego to be closer to my siblings, who were students at University of California-San Diego and San Diego State University.

After many years in Imperial Beach, my dad found work as a crane operator on a river in Bonsall, just outside San Diego. We moved to Bonsall and lived at a church retreat, a lonely, rural existence with plenty of outdoor space for kids to play. Family tensions were high at this time. My dad was very strict with my oldest brother, who suffered mental, physical, and emotional trauma that affected their relationship forever. Though my dad was an incredibly loving man, dedicated to his family, he was no saint. He was not shy about picking up a belt and often locked my brother in his room for indefinite periods. Life around the house was not fun or easy for any of us during our early, formative years, but I believe everything he did was with good intention and deemed necessary for our survival.

After a few years, Dad's job dried up, and he found himself unemployed again. His shaken integrity and inability to provide for his family—the testament of a Mexican man—buried him in a deep, year-long depression. He needed a change, and he decided to go to Mexico and camp on the beaches to focus on his health. He could not provide for his family if his body and mind were compromised, so he and my mom spent the next two years on the road, searching for an ideal place for his recovery. They found that place in Puerto Escondido, a beautiful, desolate fishing village in the state of Oaxaca, almost as far south as you can go in Mexico.

For the next two years, my mom recalls, my dad would take long walks on the beautiful, virgin beaches and return exhausted, falling into a deep sleep. He was doing what he had to do to conquer his mind and dissipate the control it had over him. He was learning the mind/body connection and realized he had to use his body to make his mind feel better. I recently found one of his letters titled, "*la belleza de mis sueños*" ("the beauty of my dreams"), in which he talks about his dreams being a driving force carrying him through his many adversities. Despite the traumatic events of his life, his dreams were always beautiful; he would dream of his ranch, his parents, and his siblings. He cherished his dreams to the point of asking himself in one of his writings, "Can a man live on dreams alone?" Perhaps this is why he would tire himself out day after day—so he could return to his ranch and visit his parents as he slept.

My brother and I lived with my oldest sister in Oxnard, California for a year and then with my oldest brother in Linda Vista, California, while my parents were in Mexico, a decision my mom was adamantly against. My brother and sister were not in a position to take care of my brother and me, and the fallout has been strained relationships ever since. This seems like an irresponsible decision, but after learning about my dad's depression and history, I understand he had no choice. He did what he had to do for his own survival and the survival of his family. When my parents finally returned, my dad was back in action, but the trauma we endured during those two years defined how we would deal with life and how we would relate to each other for the rest of our lives.

For the second time in his life, my dad was knocked down and picked himself back up. He returned this time with a vengeance, letting nothing wipe the smile off his face or get in the way of his rekindled lust for life. I don't know when it happened, but somehow, somewhere, he adopted the name El Hombre Feliz ("The Happy Man"), because you would never see him without his huge smile and bolstering laugh. People instantly fell in love with his charismatic ways and funny sayings. He was always joking around and never stopped exercising, never stopped his health practices. He kept a punching bag in the garage that he would punch for hours on end, breathing heavily and bursting out in animalistic grunts. We would tell friends he was scaring the evil spirits away. He called his health practices "tune-ups." Now that I have developed my own very similar morning routine, minus the grunting, I see why. My morning routine is a necessary part of my day to get my mind and body into their optimal state; the term couldn't be more fitting.

My dad fostered an undying passion for life and nature. Since my brothers and I were very young, he would take us on long nature walks as he hunted for food and small animals to bring back home, which at the time was torturous for teenage boys. He would capture small rabbits, birds, and even stray dogs as pets; his love for animals was enormous. He felt at home in nature; it brought him peace after years of spiraling down the rabbit hole of depression. Nature reset and grounded him. In my favorite picture of him, he's standing near the summit of the Popocatepetl volcano, just outside of Mexico City, during a family excursion up the mountain. I remember this trip vividly because of the monumental climb with my brothers, cousins, and friends, many of them strong young men in their twenties. Everyone failed to reach the summit because of altitude sickness except for my brother, my cousin, and my dad, who climbed the entire volcano barefoot. The picture embodies my dad's spirit, a huge smile on his face, doing what he loved most.

After he regained his health, as my brother and I moved on to middle school, my dad landed another job as a crane operator in Oceanside, California, where we moved in 1989. When I was in high school, I went to parties, drank, and experimented with cannabis but kept my grades consistently high until senior year, when I stopped caring about school. I was surrounded by friends who didn't care much about their grades, either, illustrating a valuable lesson I would learn later in life—that you are the average of who you associate with the most.

I took a year off after I graduated high school, following my tribe. I was working at a coffee shop when my older brother called to tell me Dad had had an accident at work. At the hospital, I learned he had lost his arm while greasing the gears of his giant crane. His hand had gotten caught in the gears, which quickly began devouring him. Reacting quickly and swiftly with astonishing might, he ripped his own arm off at the elbow and walked 100 meters to the office to call 911 because it was a Saturday and he was the only one working. The next thing he remembers is waking up in the hospital surrounded by crying family. He looked up at all of us and said, "*Quien se murió?*" ('Who died?") and laughed. This is the man my father had become. He wasn't going to let anything defeat his mind again. So, Stoicism isn't new to me at all. I have been in the midst of it my entire life.

My dad rehabilitated his arm with aloe vera, heat, and ice therapy. He learned to write with his left hand and went about life as if nothing had happened. He continued his morning "tune-ups," punching the bag now with his left fist and right elbow. This accident didn't slow him down one bit. He ran half marathons, and a newspaper wrote an article about him—the only one-armed man in his seventies running barefoot.

I was surfing in Hawaii during the summer of 2001 when I received another distressing call about my father. He had suffered a major stroke and lost the ability to move the left side of his body as well as his speech. This time it seemed life had finally gotten him. How could he recover from such a massive stroke? But, just as with his arm, he recovered his speech and started walking long distances again within a year. He continued to smile and laugh and was very self-sufficient for many years until a series of subsequent strokes rendered him bedridden for the next fifteen years.

My sister and my mom became his primary caretakers and took good care of him for the rest of his life. During those years, I don't recall ever visiting him when he wasn't smiling, laughing, joking, or singing. His classic answer to "how are you doing?" was, "*mejor que ayer, pero peor que mañana*" ("better than yesterday, but worse than tomorrow") or "*feliz de haber nacido*" ("happy to have been born"). The Marcus Aurelius quote I read every morning-- "when you arise in the morning, think of what a precious privilege it is to be alive, to breathe, to think, to enjoy, to love"—reminds me of my dad during that time

It seemed he was invincible. Nothing could bring him down; nothing could faze him. But on April 10, 2017, the day after I retreated to my brother's apartment after my life fell apart, we received the last distressing call about my dad. He had suffered another major stroke, his last. For the next ten days, his body shut down as an endless stream of relatives, friends, and so many fans came by to say goodbye. At one point, the doctor said he would probably leave his body within a few hours. He survived three more days. On April 20, a date that will always be symbolic to me in a much different way than it was in my youth, he took his last breath of air. Leopoldo Urias fought to the bitter end and never stopped smiling until he lost consciousness a few days before he passed.

My dad had started writing a book during my freshman year in high school, working diligently on it for years in our garage. We were aware of it, but he didn't speak much of it. We didn't pay much attention because we were all busy with our own lives and were oblivious to the wealth of knowledge he attained. He worked on it until he was bedridden and it became too difficult to finish. His work remains in a box somewhere in his belongings, but much of it may have been lost. It is my intention to find his work and have it printed, but for now I can only speculate. What was it that he wanted to share with the world? Perhaps stories of his youth, of his days at the ranch? Perhaps a book about health? About overcoming depression? It's very plausible this is exactly what he was writing about. He was an example of health, happiness, and virtue for the world to follow. Perhaps this was his effort to share his joy with the world.

Several times I have gone into deep meditation about this and felt connected to him, to his mission. On several occasions, I've felt his presence manifest in uncontrollable laughter in the midst of a deep WHM breathing session. I am certain his life lessons have been passed on to me, that I am following his path and continuing his mission of showing the world the immense power we hold in our bodies and minds and the incredible power in nature. It is very plausible that I'm finishing what he started over two decades ago.

THE VISION

A writer — and, I believe, generally all persons — must think that whatever happens to him or her is a resource. All things have been given to us for a purpose, and an artist must feel this more intensely. All that happens to us, including our humiliations, our misfortunes, our embarrassments, all is given to us as raw material, as clay, so that we may shape our art.
~ *Jorge Luis Borges*

The fire raged under the starlit sky at a friend's New Year's Eve party just outside Joshua Tree National Park in the high California desert. In the midst of a follow-up mushroom journey one week after my liberating beach walk with my brother, I held my new Marcus Aurelius coin and read the words, "You could leave life right now." The message rippled through my body as the skull on the front morphed into my late father's head. It was oddly appropriate. The skull resembled my dad's large, bald, round forehead, which I liked to rub and kiss when I visited him in the nursing home during his last years. I would learn over the course of this journey just how Stoic my dad was and how this coin would come to symbolize his strength. I felt connected to him as well as to Marcus Aurelius as they spoke to me, collapsing time and matter into pure energy, like they were sitting next to me at the fire revealing the secrets of the universe. It felt as if the words on the coin had just been written by Aurelius' own hand in Sirmium, present-day Serbia, where it is believed he wrote large portions of *The Meditations*. I was transported back 2,000 years, absorbing his words. I could leave life right now. Let that determine what I do, and say, and think. Opportunity was kicking down my doors.

Here I was, one hour before the new year, tightly fused to the universe with my dad and Aurelius in my pocket as my personal mentors, a clean mental slate, an operating system (Stoicism) to follow through life's inevitable adversities, and an endorphin-producing breathing technique (WHM) that obliterated all my stress, worries, and anxieties. I was finally free; the universe had gifted me three incredibly powerful tools, and the world was my playground again. I asked myself, "If I could leave life right now, what is the last thing I would want to do?" That was an easy question to answer. Ever since I moved to Germany when I was nineteen, my passion, my true love, has been skiing deep powder on big mountains. I decided then and there that I would move to Lake Tahoe and return to my true love: the mountains, snow, and nature. The idea felt completely right.

A few days later, I began preparing for the move and realized I had never unpacked when I arrived from Mexico ten months earlier. I hadn't wanted to see any of my belongings, worried they would trigger negative emotions. Now, full of energy, highly focused, thinking clearly, and listening to music for the first time in months, I reorganized all my belongings (not all that many, by design), and arrived in Lake Tahoe two weeks later—free of antidepressants, sleeping well again, with healthy digestion again after the meds had wreaked havoc on my body, triggering chronic diarrhea and insomnia.

For the next two months, I hit the mountain almost every day; practiced WHM, complete with ice showers; and followed my yoga routine. I started microdosing a tiny amount of psilocybin mushrooms every three or four days, but quickly realized WHM was giving me everything I needed. I didn't need the mushrooms because consistently practicing WHM is a type of endogenous microdosing. The torture of reliving the day my wife left was gone, but sometimes a song on the radio would remind me of my life in Mexico, and I would have to drown out the negativity with a few rounds of Wim Hof breathing.

My newfound happiness and resilience were tested two months later when my three job prospects in Lake Tahoe fell through and I had to develop a contingency plan. This would have been disastrous if I hadn't had WHM to snap me out of my fear and malaise. I was able to see that darkness is not to be feared because the abyss is where strength, resilience, and fortitude are found. I remained strong and happy to engage in whatever fate had in store for me, to view this new challenge as a blessing. I decided to go to Mexico, where it's much less expensive to live, and surf for two months, then I returned to San Diego for a second ear surgery, which completely restored my hearing and reconnected me with the world. Nothing could phase me now. I spent the rest of that summer surfing in San Diego before returning to Lake Tahoe to ski and work the winter season on the mountain with ski patrol, a lifelong dream.

For the next six months, I continued my practice and routine, spending every day watching the sun rise over Lake Tahoe from my skis during one of the snowiest winters the lake had seen in years. When the snow finally stopped falling, I went back to Mexico film a documentary about my journey with a friend, spending two months traveling from the beaches of Puerto Escondido through the southern highlands of Oaxaca to the majestic colonial capital city of Oaxaca, to ancient Puebla and the vibrant, culturally rich metropolis of Mexico City. It was the most important, educational, and enlightening adventure of my life.

One day, while staying with my friend Camilla on an organic farm in the mountains just outside the magical little town of San Jose del Pacifico, Oaxaca, I took a *temascal*, a traditional sauna dug into the mineral-rich red earth, then drank some mushroom tea and lay down on my bed, eyes closed, listening to a meditation playlist curated for my journey. My intention was to visit and resolve any remaining demons, residual pain, animosity, or depression stuck inside me. It had been a year and a half since the first mushroom journey that saved my life. I had been ecstatic ever since, and my life was so incredible that I felt like it had all been resolved. But how could it? That seemed too easy and too quick.

Everything started to dissipate as my body dissolved effortlessly, and I was slowly reduced to nothing. I couldn't tell where I ended and the universe began. I couldn't tell if I still had a body. Every fiber of my being extended out into the furthest reaches of the universe. I was breathing, so I had lungs, but these two distinguishable elements of myself, my consciousness and my body morphed into mere ideas and then into pure energy. I was reduced to simply oxygen and carbon dioxide as I inhaled and exhaled. There was no need for a body, for anything at all. Was I dead? I thought this must be where we go when we die. It all made sense in this realm that I can't quite describe. It just was. So much peace and euphoria; I was perfectly content. I wanted to stay here. So much pain, suffering, and struggle on Earth. If this is where we go, why would anyone fear death? It was all so beautiful!

I saw the collection of memories and emotions that make up Gerardo and began to disassemble myself, viewing every emotion I'd ever had, positive and negative, as different components of myself. My anger was a section of me, as was sadness, loneliness, happiness, and joy. I isolated my ego, converted the voice into a tangible entity, and silenced it. For the first time in my life, I could easily stop the inner monologue and co-exist with it in silence as it floated next to me in space.

After about ten minutes (truthfully, who knows how long) of floating in space as disassembled Gerardo, as oxygen and carbon dioxide, I opened my eyes. Holy hell! What the...? I liked it better out there, in the farthest corner of the universe. Back on Earth, in Mexico, on my bed in our handmade clay cabin with horses outside our front window, all the difficulties of living on planet Earth—gravity, using this body—hit me like a brick wall. I felt like an alien in a new meat bag trying to learn the laws of Earthly physics. I realized all pain and suffering is an inherent part of the human form, the cost of having this body, this vehicle—the price of life. It's so much easier out there as pure consciousness, devoid of pain and suffering. I got it! I precisely got it! There was nothing to fear!

I spent the rest of the journey either floating around feeling absolute bliss, eyes closed, or struggling to move around in this meat bag, eyes open, having to use the toilet and trivial human difficulties of that nature (what a hassle). I then visited my family, one by one, exploring any sadness for the problems that plagued us. I tried to find residual anger or depression from my divorce, any grief from my dad's death, fear about my mom's inevitable end of life.

I was struck by an extraordinary feeling; I couldn't find the darkness. The euphoria and level of understanding I found about everything that has ever existed was so overwhelming that any dark thoughts seemed like what they truly are: illusions. Is this the true essence of existence? Bliss, love, and tranquility? How could I be sad that my mom is nearing the end of her life? She has lived a courageous, incredible eighty-four years against countless odds and is still kicking! Longevity runs in our blood. What a blessing! She raised six children with nothing in two countries! What a hero! She is so strong and wise. In this intense psychedelic realm, death becomes neutralized into an inherent part of the process of life which wouldn't exist if it were not for death. Death becomes beautiful. As Alan Watts has said, "death implies life."

After exploring this realm, I tried a few rounds of Wim Hof breathing, which hyper-blasted me out into space, an intense euphoria engulfing my entire body, lights and patterns dancing behind my eyelids, surely flooding my brain with DMT. A deep knowing emanated from within. I could time travel; I could see the future and the past. I saw my entire ancestry, from the evolution of our early hominids to the Aztecs who occupied Mexico to the Tarahumara winning marathons barefoot. I saw these indigenous men running a marathon, carrying a torch and passing it forward to their youth for many generations, then on to my grandpa, and then to my dad, running barefoot. My dad reached an enormous mountaintop, where I waited for him as he passed the torch on to me to continue his mission, our *lucha indigena* (indigenous struggle). The torch morphed into this book, a documentary project, this trip in Mexico. I grabbed it and ran with it.

It was the torch of ancient, sacred knowledge and wisdom that resides in the mountains, ecosystems, and indigenous peoples of Mexico, in the molecules of the psilocybin mushroom and the peyote cactus, in the poison of the *bufo alvarius* Sonoran Desert toad, in the maguey cactus that produces tequila, mescal, and pulque, the ancient Aztec "drink of the gods." How important it was for me to get this message out to the world. How lucky I was to be in my dad's country with my dad's descendants, healing my mind with life-saving plant medicines, working on this documentary with the locals, plant medicine experts, curanderos, shamans, scientists, and mycologists. How lucky I was to be alive on this path. How lucky I was that tragedy struck me so hard that it propelled me in a direction I would have never imagined.

After my ego-dissolving journey in the mountains, I knew I had to figure out how I could help the most people in the quickest and most effective way possible. The question I always ask myself when faced with a big task is, what would this look like if it were easy? We tend to overcomplicate things, coming up with everything that could possibly go wrong. So, my vision developed. I'm publishing this book to make what I've learned accessible to people all over the world who can benefit from it. A percentage of the proceeds will go to a foundation that will focus on two objectives: funding psychedelic research and developing psychedelic treatment centers where people can receive psychedelic therapy and immerse in yoga, breathing techniques, saunas and ice baths, and outdoor activities in a natural setting. This is my vision.

If I could turn my entire life around so abruptly, so astonishingly quickly, anyone can. I hope to motivate others who are suffering as I was. After I began writing this book and journaling daily, I began to feel as if I were living in the book's pages. What I do today, I will write about tonight. What I do tomorrow will be part of the journey. This book is my story; I am the producer and main character. Why not choose to do amazing things? Why not choose to think amazing thoughts? Why not choose an amazing story? It's all in my control. I once heard a conversation on the radio in which someone said, "When you own your story, you get to write your own ending." I'm writing my own ending.

My intention is to reach others who are suffering as I was and show them there is another way—to tell the world a real story of a person at the end of his rope, ready to give it all up, before everything changed overnight. This is my self-guide, my blueprint out of depression, and my attempt to raise awareness for the plant medicines, therapies, practices, and philosophies that saved my life. What started as a magical journey out of severe depression continues to morph into an insatiable thirst for knowledge, enlightenment, self-discovery, awareness, improvement, and a growing desire to help others. It has led me to discover unimaginable things about myself and sparked a curiosity about life and the universe that I'd never had.

I'm exploring my family lineage and learning astonishing things along the way, like my father having the intuition, foresight, and courage to flee the ranch where he was raised in the mountains of Sinaloa, the present-day Golden Triangle of northern Mexico, where the Tarahumara Indians, my surviving ancestors (those who were not as lucky as my dad) are left with little choice but to cultivate cannabis and opium poppy plants. With my dad's departure from his ranch, as much as it pained him to leave, he evaded the drug wars that are ravishing Mexico today, a life my family was destined to live if it weren't for my dad's courage. *Gracias, Papi!*

It is time we liberate ourselves from the prison of our minds and awaken to reality, not only to overcome trauma and depression, but to thrive as a species. To infuse our lives with joy so we can share that joy, spreading the ripple, and actively help make the world a better place. "We change the world not by what we say or do, but as a consequence of what we have become." I have read this quote by the late David R. Hawkins every day since December 22, 2017. It starts with the individual, from within. We have all the tools we need within us and in nature to live the best life we can possibly imagine. It's time to explore our own consciousness; it's time to look inward for answers. As Jason Silva says, "The new space is inner space." It is time to evolve.

There will be a day when neglecting self-awareness, self-improvement, emotional control, and transcendence of the ego through a mental discipline of some sort and/or with the use of psychedelics will be seen as primitive, as willfully staying blind to the greater consciousness, willfully limiting our awareness, clinging to our identities as primates controlled by our destructive ego and emotions, which is destructive for society and the world at large. It will be compared to the time when we did not wash our hands before medical procedures–not so long ago.

It is my hope that my story reaches as many people as possible, that this knowledge is passed on, and that we collectively educate, motivate, and support each other. Let's vote; let's change the laws. Just as one snowflake after another can cause a devastating avalanche, word of mouth can ultimately change the world. Let's give our loved ones who are suffering not only a chance for mental freedom, but a chance to thrive–to be happier, healthier, and stronger than they've ever been. Help us make the world a better place, one person at a time. It all starts from within, right here, right now, in this present moment.

We all have a story. Depression only means a sad story has been written. But we are the authors of our stories. My story was once tragic, but today it is the story of my beautiful, magical transformation, my awakening, my transcendence. The "tragic" events of 2017 now represent my strength and resilience. They represent freedom, happiness, health, and true, lasting, inner peace that resides inside each of us. I simply changed the narrative, the significance of these events. I rewrote history; we can do that. It's never too late to change your story. Just as a sailboat leaves a wake but the wake does not determine the boat's direction, the stories we tell ourselves about our past do not have to determine our direction. We can leave them in our wake. We can change the position of the sails at any time and steer our boat in any direction we want.

I hope I have illustrated that all suffering is simply an abstraction of the mind, a story fueled by the ego, which lives in the past and the future, both of which are mere illusions. As Eckhart Tolle says in *The Power of Now*, "In the present moment lies your freedom." I have laid out the path I took and the tools I have used and continue using in hopes that others suffering can make use of this information to achieve presence, to achieve freedom. Nature provides us with everything we need to be "happy, healthy, and strong," as the Iceman says. Choose which tools work for you, combine them, experiment with them, use them all, like I do, or find new tools and share your story with the world.

No matter who you are or what you do, your story affects everyone and everything around you; your story has consequences. Remember that our actions, no matter how small, have a ripple effect on the entire universe forever. "Whatever happens to you has been waiting to happen since the beginning of time," Marcus Aurelius said. "The twining strands of fate wove both of them together: your own existence and the things that happen to you."

As a wave does not stand alone, we are also the product of the entire universe and its activity since the beginning of time. When we watch a wave, we are watching the activity of all the ocean's water molecules on Earth, which give birth to the wave. As such, we all have an effect on the universe every moment of our existence. Any feelings of isolation are mere illusions, stories of the ego. As Alan Watts, the late British-American philosopher, so beautifully describes in his lectures, we tend to view ourselves as strangers to the world, as independent agents on an independent mission, as "something that has arrived here by fluke." We believe there is us and there is the world, but this is an illusion, just like the wave.

"What we are basically, deep, deep down, far, far in, is simply the fabric and structure of existence itself," Watts says.[108] We were created by planet Earth and by the universe to perceive life by way of a sensory apparatus occurring in every cell in our body, in every sensation. Therefore, what is happening outside of us is precisely what is happening inside of us, inside our brains, in our nervous system. Our thoughts create our perceptions of the world, which literally and scientifically create our reality. As Dr. Gabor Mate says in the film *The Wisdom of Trauma* (thewisdomeoftrauma.com), "The state of our physiology determines our view of the world." Whatever reality you see before your eyes in this very moment is malleable. It is clay; it is mere perception. The time is now, and time is all we have.

In the words of Marcus Aurelius, "Everything is only for a day. Confine yourself to the present." So, go ahead, pick up a pen. How do you want your story to end?

My dad about to summit the iconic 5,426-meter active Popocatépetl volcano just outside of Mexico City. Our climbing team consisted of friends and family, mostly strong, young men in their twenties and thirties, fully equipped with boots and all the necessary gear. Papi, barefoot, out-climbed all of them and was one of only three who made it to the summit. The rest, myself included, had to turn back because of altitude sickness. This is my favorite picture of my dad as it embodies his spirit and what he lived for.

My dad running a half marathon in Tijuana, Mexico, barefoot at 70 years old. He was a mad man.

ADDENDA

BULLETPROOF ROUTINE

The only reason I'm able to maintain an elevated baseline of strength, happiness, gratitude, and joy on a daily basis is because of this routine, these practices, and this ongoing training.

I like to think of life as a sport. Every day is a new game with new players but the objective remains, or at least it should, the same: How can we make the world a better place? Through this daily routine, this daily training, I can take on the day in the most optimal manner, with strength, calm, a level head, and most importantly, joy.

I fill my body and brain with nutrient-rich food and plenty of oxygen before I start my day, just as we take care of our car and fill the gas tank before embarking on a road trip. Just like a car, neglecting necessary maintenance of our body and mind will eventually result in an inevitable breakdown. I do this so I can be a positive force for those around me who may not train for this sport of life and suffer as a result, so I don't react negatively to situations I have no control over (most situations), so I can catch my mind before it starts making assumptions and taking things personally, so I can lead this tango of life instead of reactively following. This routine enables me to make better decisions rooted in the present moment. It's a very sustainable system. Air, nutritious food, and water are all we really require in life. Everything else is extra. Health is wealth.

So, if life is a sport, why not play in the Olympics and give it everything you've got? It actually becomes quite fun seeing just how much you can improve yourself. (Always check with your physician or health practitioner before making any diet or exercise changes.)

6 a.m.: Wake up, make the bed

If you make your bed first thing every morning, you will have accomplished the first task of the day. It will give you a small sense of pride and will encourage you to do another task, and another, and another. It is a psychological trick to spark motivation. In addition to this, keeping your room clean and organized is very important. A cluttered environment leads to a cluttered mind, and vice versa.

A note about minimalism from Anaïs Nin: "In order to change skins, evolve into new cycles, I feel one has to learn to discard. If one changes internally, one should not continue to live with the same objects. They reflect one's mind and psyche of yesterday. I throw away what has no dynamic, living use."

30-40 minutes of yoga

Now, pull out the yoga mat and stop the mind from thinking. The trick here is to get a head start in the daily race against our mind, which is very quick to the starting line. We have to train ourselves to gain that split-second advantage from the beginning. When we do, we can create the course we will be racing for the day and lead the way. When I skip this step, I feel like I'm catching up all day.

I practice thirty to forty minutes of a personalized yoga routine. This can be suited to your taste. Because I ski and surf a lot, I have developed a routine that focuses heavily on stretching. Memorize it so the mind can go deeper into the body and out of the head by means of muscle memory, or autopilot. I like to throw in some fire breaths, a quick abdominal organ massage and some face stretching. We have forty-three muscles in our faces, and all of them communicate with our minds regarding our mood. This is especially useful in the morning when we wake up in a funky mood because of our dreams. We can disrupt the facial muscle feedback system and signal to our brain that everything is okay. The goal is to awaken our body's innate physical intelligence and bring the mind and body together.

15-minute Wim Hof deep breathing session

I "get high on my own supply" while lying down. After that, I lie there and enjoy the endorphins, cannabinoids, opioids, and DMT that just blasted throughout my body and brain.

10-minute meditation

Just breathe and connect with the body. When I finish my meditation and open my eyes, I repeat this Marcus Aurelius quote to myself:

Think of yourself as dead. You have lived your life. Now take what's left and live it properly.

Memento mori, always. With practice, death becomes fuel for gratitude.

Ice bath or cold shower

Boost your immune system. Calm your mind. Feel great.

Nutrition

It is impossible to overestimate the relevance of nutrition when it comes to our physical, emotional, and mental well-being. While my diet is ever evolving, I focus on eating organic, whole foods and drinking clean, spring water if possible, with a focus on fermented foods.

At least 70 percent of our immune system is modulated in our gut, which also harbors 95 percent of our serotonin, vitally important for our mental and emotional well-being.[109] Take care of your gut, and it will take care of you.

I believe the optimal diet is varied and very biospecific to each person, so this is an individual culinary journey.

Outdoor activity and morning sunshine

Recent studies have shown that direct exposure to early morning sunlight increases serotonin, which is directly correlated with mood regulation and produces melatonin, essential for sleep (quality, deep sleep is essential for health).[110] Dr. Andrew Huberman, a neurobiologist and ophthalmologist at Stanford University, says early exposure to sunlight resets our circadian rhythm and kicks off a host of metabolic functions to produce energy for the day. In a nutshell, the more sunshine you get, the better you will feel and the better you will sleep.

My favorite activities on earth are surfing, skiing, and rock climbing, but when I'm not lucky enough to be doing one of these, a quick barefoot walk on the beach or in a park will suffice. The point is to get your body moving and get some of that delicious, life-creating sunlight and fresh oxygen. Keep feeding the engine. Pay attention to the emerging science on "grounding" to learn why barefoot walks are beneficial. My dad knew what he was doing. A *Journal of Inflammation Research* paper reports, "Grounding appears to improve sleep, normalize the day–night cortisol rhythm, reduce pain, reduce stress, shift the autonomic nervous system from sympathetic toward parasympathetic activation, increase heart rate variability, speed wound healing, and reduce blood viscosity."[111]

Journal

Journaling is one of the most powerful and effective ways to initiate change. The Stoics knew what they were doing.

Read a few quotes

When you arise in the morning, think of what a precious privilege it is to be alive — to breathe, to think, to enjoy, to love.
~ *Marcus Aurelius*

Waking up to who you are requires letting go of who you imagine yourself to be.
~ *Alan Watts*

Confine yourself to the present.
~*Marcus Aurelius*

To-do list

At the top of the to-do list on my phone—the first thing on my list to accomplish every day—is a picture of this mantra I saw and loved right after a chakra clearing/yoga/meditation session.

Every day, think as you wake up, today I am fortunate to have woken up. I am alive. I have a precious human life. I am not going to waste it. I am going to use all my energies to develop myself, to expand my heart out to others, to achieve enlightenment for the benefit of all beings. I am going to have kind thoughts towards others. I am not going to get angry or think badly about others. I am going to benefit others as much as I can.
~ *The XIVth Dali Lama*

Next, I visualize my goals for the next year as if they have already happened. I find that by doing this, my vision becomes clearer, and I am able to merge that vision with reality more fluidly. Dr. Joe Dispenza, author of *Breaking the Habit of Being Yourself* and *Becoming Supernatural*, says that by feeling the emotions of our desired future, we draw the elements of that future from the quantum field towards us, which materializes in coincidences, opportunities, and synchronicities.

Eat well, manage stress

When it comes to food, I try to be mindful of what I am putting in my body and stick to whole, organic foods. I try to stay in ketosis, a metabolic state in which the body converts fat into ketones to use as its main source of energy. By shifting from glucose metabolism to fat metabolism, I bypass the need to run on glucose. Ketones are a more efficient source of energy than glucose and have numerous health benefits.[112] Navy Seals have long used ketosis during missions to achieve longer breath holds underwater and prevent underwater seizures.[113] When in ketosis, I experience a noticeable improvement in mental clarity as well as an overall euphoric feeling in my body, a clean energy. Ketosis helps me control my blood glucose levels because I have diabetes, but everyone is different and should do their own research.

I also intermittently fast daily and try to do an extended fast every few months for the numerous powerful health benefits correlated with fasting, including glucose control, boosted immune system, increased energy levels, mental clarity, and increased autophagy. My dad was a huge fan of fasting and was very healthy his entire life.

If and when I feel stressed, I stop whatever I'm doing, relax, sit down, and take several deep breaths and very slowly hum them out through my nose. I try to take three breaths or less per minute. In a few minutes I feel better. If I have more time, I do a round of Wim Hof breathing.

Before bed: Journal, review the day

I will keep a constant watch over myself and, most usefully, will put each day up for review. For this is what makes us evil — that none of us looks back upon our own lives. We reflect upon only that which we are about to do. And yet our plans for the future descend from the past.

~ Seneca

Sleep well, maintain healthy circadian rhythm

I do this by viewing early sunlight and getting plenty of sunlight throughout the day; exercising; avoiding caffeine and alcohol; keeping healthy sleep habits; maintaining a clean, organized home; and practicing yoga and meditation. Lack of quality sleep is extremely detrimental to our health.[114] Conversely, deep, quality sleep is one of the most effective ways of improving our health. Ensuring optimal sleep is the only way to ensure an optimal day. Your day starts with last night's decisions. Do what you must to get solid sleep.

Long-term stress management

I continue to use psychedelics for long-term stress management a few times per year. When that creeping, slow buildup of stress and anxiety starts to accumulate in my body, I wipe the mental slate clean and refresh my mind with a tune-up and reboot for the mind and soul. Altered states of consciousness offer us the unique opportunity to step outside of ourselves and view ourselves from a different angle. Just as a sports team watches the game on the screen to improve their game, altered states of consciousness, be it through meditation, yoga, breath work, or psychedelics, offer us the same opportunity to spot any dysfunctions, traumas (we all have trauma; being born is a trauma),[115] or blind spots we do not see in daily life that contribute to our stress so we can address them.

CASE STUDIES

Psychedelics

I'm one of thousands of people whose lives have been saved and dramatically enhanced by psychedelics. You may have heard that both Steve Jobs and Bill Gates claimed to have experimented with psychedelics or that, more recently, Mike Tyson said "toad venom," which contains the psychedelic compound 5-MeO-DMT, changed his life. "The toad is a totally interesting aspect of my whole being now," Tyson said. "It takes you to a place that takes you to another dimension. Ever since I did it, I've had a miraculous change about me."[116]

Psychedelics influenced the lives of many famous musicians, artists, poets, and authors who transformed the societal, cultural, and political landscape of the 1960s, and the lives of countless ordinary people have also been affected in miraculous ways. Here's what a few people have had to say, via Psychedelic Insights and Safe Spaces Amsterdam, two legal psychedelic therapy facilities located in Amsterdam, Netherlands:[117]

"I witnessed my negative thoughts and how these were keeping me down. I can change it now. This feels like oxygen for the soul. I can breathe again."
~ Anonymous

"I saw myself through the eyes of love. I needed that."
~ Anonymous

"I laughed so much I will forever be reminded not to take life so seriously."
~ Anonymous

"I felt I was loved and I am here to love in return."
~ Anonymous

"I kept convincing myself that I was so small and unimportant. No more. I've seen it."
~ Anonymous

"Psilocybin has been an exceptional teacher. It has opened the doors of perception further than I've ever experienced before. Nothing compares, all my studies of philosophy and religion, my deepest introspective meditations or hours in isolation tank sessions don't even come close. I feel renewed with a fresh sense of optimism and a genuine love of life. It has really helped my depression and anxiety issues immensely. Mission accomplished! We can't control the world, but we can control how we feel about it."
~ Anonymous

"I feel extremely happy for the opportunity to experience something so profound that it made me question the nature of reality and our place in it. I believe it's human nature to be drawn to the unanswerable questions of our origins and the meaning behind it all. By no means do I have all the answers, but I feel an incredible amount of relief to experience just a tiny piece of it. One of my favorite insights that I came back with was the knowledge that the true nature of the universe is infinitely more beautiful than what we can perceive with our default neural filter. It's almost like psilocybin polishes that 'window of consciousness,' as you put it, making things look clear."
~ Anonymous

"This experience was exactly what I needed. The trip was a very profound, almost religious journey, which gave me handles to use in the real world. I'm able to give love, instead of just receiving. Whatever the future has in store for me, I know I can change now, and that is definitive. Ten years of psychotherapy could not have made this happen."

~ Anonymous

"I really cannot begin to express how meaningful the entire experience was."

~ Anonymous

"I still have trouble putting my experience into words, but I would say it has changed my life. During my experience, I 'saw' the entire universe and understood my place in it. I saw what matters. I saw my birth, and my death, and realized there is nothing to fear. I am an atheist, but I felt and saw what could be interpreted as God. I have never felt anything so beautiful. To say that I cried and laughed would be an understatement, for several hours I was totally overwhelmed by beauty and awe for our universe and the people and animals in it. I also had a deep moment of feeling my mind growing, my consciousness expanded to include new ways of viewing and understanding my life."

~ Anonymous

"When I got back from Afghanistan, I was still, every day for years, in Afghanistan. I was still looking for threats and IEDs, still hypervigilant and on constantly. I remember during my first [MDMA] treatment thinking to myself, I think I can leave Afghanistan in the past now, and now, I wake up, and I'm home. I'm not in Afghanistan anymore, the war is not a part of my life, it's in the past and I can leave it in the past... and that's something I couldn't do for years."[118]

~ Military Psychologist and Afghanistan War Veteran

"In June of 2018, I decided to take my first journey to

Peru to work with ayahuasca for ten days in the jungle. It's crazy that it took me that long, as I had known about the work with plant medicine for about a decade but never felt ready. I experienced a lot of fear around the use of psychedelic substances, since my only experience with them was recreationally as a teenager. I struggled with depression from a very young age, and had my first major suicide attempt at age 16. It only got worse from there over the next five years. More intentional overdoses, depression, psych wards, and finally, in-patient rehab at age 23. I struggled with drug and alcohol abuse, and my life was no longer mine. It was after I went to in-patient rehab that I started to connect with spirituality. Something finally clicked, and I knew there was something bigger than myself keeping me alive after all this self destruction.

Fast forward ten years: I finally made it to the jungle and was ready to embark on what I expected to be the most transformational experience of my life; I was ready. I left fifteen days before my birthday and was slated to spend my last night in the jungle, entering into my thirty-fifth year around the sun. I kissed my partner Ryan goodbye and left for Peru.

We arrived in Pulcolpa on June 4th at the compound where we would spend the last night on the grid before ten days deep in the jungle with no contact with the outside world. That night, I spoke with my boyfriend a bit and retired for bed super early, as I was experiencing a severe migraine. I slept twelve hours that night and didn't wake up once until the next morning. I texted my boyfriend to call me, as this would be the last time we would be able to talk for the next ten days. I knew he had worked late as a bartender, so I figured he must have been sleeping, as it was about 8 a.m. We were in the van headed into the jungle when I received a text from my roommate to call her; I knew something was wrong. She told me that Ryan had died sometime last night, seemingly in his sleep. Panic and shock simultaneously took over my entire body.

We turned the van around and went back to the compound where we began to make arrangements for me to return home immediately. Nothing can ever prepare you for the tragic loss of a loved one. The road ahead was going to be long and hard.

I found the heroin Ryan had overdosed on under the sink when I got home. In hindsight, it was so obvious he was using, but I refused to see it at the time. I kept thinking if I hadn't left for the jungle, he would still be alive, and I could have helped him get clean. Guilt and grief consumed me. The first two weeks, I numbed out pretty hard and turned to alcohol and prescription drugs. I was barely coherent during his service, and highly suicidal.

About two weeks after Ryan's death, I was invited to sit in a San Pedro ceremony. I knew I needed to drop the pills if I had any chance of getting through this alive and decided to go to the ceremony to see if I could connect with Ryan and hopefully find some peace. In the ceremony, I sat next to my best friend, who was familiar with the medicine and the group. With her by my side, I was able to truly surrender and trust, knowing she was there to support me, not something I do easily with others. I also allowed myself to be supported by complete strangers, and I felt love from people I never even knew were available to me. And then suddenly, I connected with Ryan. I felt his energy in the trees and the sky around me. I clearly saw that Ryan and I had chosen each other for this path. His soul was not meant to live in his body any longer. I saw that I was meant to be his last partner in this life; I was chosen to hold the space for him as he transitioned. This was how it was written, and there was nothing to fight. This was our soul contract.

After the first San Pedro ceremony, I started weaning off the prescription meds, and began taking the additional steps to heal. I began working with kambo to detox my body, which had been under duress for many years from heavy drug and alcohol use. I started working with psilocybin to help with the depression and attended another San Pedro ceremony a few months later. In October 2018, I tried 5-Meo-DMT, which really took things to the next level, and gave me *a lot* to process for the next year! (That would be another ten paragraphs at least...)

After six months, I was completely off prescription medicine. I left my job as an alcohol representative and actually began to see a light at the end of this dark tunnel. Then, in August 2019, I finally found myself with ayahuasca again. The night before the ceremony, I had a dream in which Ryan came to me. We were lying under the stars, our energy embraced; it felt so real. In the dream, I asked him if he was going to come back. He said "no," softly. I already knew the answer, and I understood; I told him it was ok and that I would keep seeing him here.

The dream was so powerful and beautiful, and although I was still nervous, I knew he was with me. After this long, crazy relationship with ayahuasca, I had never actually ingested the medicine, and now it was time. I took what would be considered a small dose, but it was enough. I felt the emotions almost immediately. I felt the pain, the sadness, the immense trauma of that day, energetically replaying over and over. I called out to Ryan, and he said, "I'm here baby."

I cried and cried. I pushed my face down hard into the ground. I started channeling all the pain into the earth. I began to feel the release and let it out, more and more, it just kept coming. After some time, I began to feel complete. I laid with my eyes closed, with Ryan next to me, and I felt peace.

It has been about six months since my ayahuasca journey, and I have taken this time to integrate all the work I did with plant/frog medicine in those first fourteen months. I work with a coach and a group where we study non-dualism through "A Course in Miracles." This has been paramount to my integration process.

If it weren't for the experiences with plant medicine and the perspective from non-dualistic study, I don't know where I would be today on my journey. This month, I opened The Metaphysical Healing Institute of Palm Beach in Florida. I am a healthy, happy person. I have peace in my life that I never knew existed. I have recreated my relationship with my late partner, and he now holds the space of a great teacher and guide. I have accomplished things and pushed myself far beyond anything I could have done without this catalyst. I am so very grateful for these plant medicines."

~ Nicole Amelia

Wim Hof Method

The Wim Hof Method (WHM) Facebook group has over 160,000 members worldwide. These are a few of the inspiring stories of people who are overcoming very debilitating conditions with the WHM that have been told there. Some names have been changed for privacy.

"Since being diagnosed with multiple sclerosis five years ago, the Wim Hof Method has assisted me immensely. The simple yet profound aspect of deep deliberate breaths in combination with cold exposure has eradicated my pains, and has been an absolute game changer."

~ Shawn

"My first memory ever was more of a sensation than a memory, the sensation of fear. This feeling of deep fear has been a constant companion my entire life until recently. My first years of school were terrifying, never fitting in, never feeling 'normal.' As a child, I noticed that I would often get upset over things nobody else seemed to even react to and interpreted life from a very explosive, fragile, inner world. I started daydreaming a lot and avoiding uncomfortable situations. At age thirteen, I had my first psychotic episode. This was triggered by a change in schools, and an environment I wasn't mature enough to handle. No one suspected anything was wrong because I became a master at blending into the background so no one would notice me. I was regularly absent from school, always felt overwhelmed, and made up excuses to be able to miss school. I had a few really close friends, but everyone, and everything else, was a threat. I continued this pattern of avoidance and self-isolation for many years.

Despite being born into a secure, safe, loving family, I

never felt confident or safe on the inside. I was always scared and had difficulty adapting to change. Later in life, this manifested in the inability to hold a job for more than a few months at a time. Then, depression, or mania, would hit, and the cycle would start all over. I didn't know what was wrong with me. I felt, and was told by others, that I was lazy and had a poor character. I struggled with this for many years, never fitting in with society, which meant a lot of time at home, which I now see was a blessing in disguise, because it allowed me to watch my two beautiful girls grow up right in front of me. They truly are what saved my life during this time. Being a dad was the only thing that made sense to me and gave me a true purpose.

At the age of 35, I found myself at the doctor's office again. During this time, I had no self-confidence and suicide attempts became a frequent occurrence. But then, as soon as I felt the panic and depression coming, I would see my daughters in front of me, and they instantly broke the downward spiral. They balanced me and have always been my true angels. I was so ashamed of my actions, however, I never told anyone, until now.

After meeting with a psychologist and a therapist several times and many rigorous tests, both physical and mental, I was diagnosed with bipolar disorder. I began to forgive myself for trying to fight an impossible battle. It took over a year to adapt to the medication they prescribed, but I was excited to have a way out of my manic/depressive episodes. The therapy helped, and I thought my condition was improving, then one day, everything went grey, and I realized the medication had taken me from a roller coaster state of mind to a prolonged emotionless suspense. I absolutely see and recognize that therapy and medication saved me during this time, but now I wasn't dealing with life, but rather numb from the medication, without any power to act. I felt I had changed one prison for another, and my body started to revolt by creating its own numerous, and prolonged, panic attacks. Nothing had really changed; I was back to square one. I ended up in a mental hospital again, and continued to battle my mind just to keep afloat.

I had now been battling my condition for over 30 years, and was really stretched to the limit.

At the beginning of 2017, I started experiencing something called "mixed state," an explosion of both depressive and hypomanic emotions that would pop up several times a day. Like a roller coaster without breaks, it took me on a journey of inner turmoil and chaos. This mental state continued until one day I suddenly found myself in a strange vacuum with an eerie silence within. Over the next few weeks, I did some introspective searching, and it was during this time that I heard about a man who, through painful personal tragedy and hardships, had found a way to heal himself through nature. This resonated deeply with me. The prospect of using natural tools like breathing, cold exposure, and building strength from within sounded amazing. It spoke to me on every level, and I connected deeply with his life story; his name was Wim Hof. Learning about his story and the method he had built for over thirty years, which I now had a chance to be a part of, made me fall to the floor crying. After three decades of searching, I finally felt I had found the tools to heal myself. Wim showed me a flicker of light, and I grabbed on to it like my life depended on it. I started with a daily regimen of waking up early to do three rounds of breathing and push-ups and started taking cold showers. It took me about three weeks to have my first real positive experience, and it was a powerful and unexpected one. A few days later, coming out of my cold shower, I realized something amazing. I rushed downstairs, into the kitchen where my parents, my ex- wife, and our two daughters were having breakfast, and, bursting with excitement, I exclaimed, "It's amazing! I can see colors! I actually see everything in bright color!" Something had clicked, and I regained color vision. The constant haze was gone; it was bewildering.

I soon found myself in Stockholm, Sweden, at a Wim Hof Method workshop, getting into my first proper ice bath. All the adversity I had experienced up to this moment completely vanished when I sat in that freezing cold water. No bad memories, feelings, or soul crushing pain existed; I was mentally naked, but not for one second did I feel vulnerable or exposed. It was here in the ice that I saw myself for the first time without the protective armor and defensive walls I had built my whole life. I felt like an open book without any written content, ready to create my life from scratch.

I combined my newfound training regimen with my love for nature in the vast green Swedish forests, swift running rivers, deep lakes, and cold Baltic Sea, and exposed myself to life. At last, I was captain of my own ship.

A few days after my forty-fourth birthday, I found myself in a group with like-minded people at Wim Hof's personal home in Stroe, Holland, embarking on the Masters Week in Poland. We spent a deeply transformative week high in the Polish mountains, where everything I believed about myself was challenged. Together, as a group, we came together as one. We overcame incredible individual and group challenges, and after this humbling week that presented many obstacles (this could be an entire book in itself!), I finally became a certified Wim Hof Method instructor!

I don't know where I would be today if it weren't for Wim Hof and his method. By applying this method to my life, I have been able to break free from isolation, depression, pain, and fear. Through breathing exercises and cold exposure, I've created space between depression and mania, and in this space, I am able to find myself. Exterior triggers and negativity have no permanent hold over me anymore because I am more in control of my emotions. Step by step, in collaboration with my doctors,

I've removed almost all the medication I had been taking for years. I am learning to become my own healer by being more open and conscious in life and trusting and believing in myself. It is my mission to help others pave the road back to their health by teaching them to tap into their inner power. It is with a warm heart that I thank everyone who has been a part of my journey."

~ Andreas Gustafsson
Certified WHM Instructor

"Rejection sensitivity dysphoria (RSD) feels like a tsunami of mental and even physical pain that hits out of nowhere, typically when my mood is laid-back, relaxed, and go-with-the-flow. When I [would] perceive that I had been rejected, or criticized, especially by someone I know, the storm would come. I might have run or walked away swiftly, isolated myself, cried uncontrollably, even hurt myself sometimes. It would be very intense, but when it was over, I would hold no grudges and would be able to go back to 'normal.' It is something I've struggled with my whole life. When I was a little kid, my parents said I would bang my head on the floor whenever I was in trouble. It didn't matter if I was at work, home, school, or with my wonderful husband. My behavior would be less than ideal and even put me in dangerous and embarrassing situations when a storm of RSD would strike, even at my bachelorette party and wedding last year! Enough was enough. I thought for sure I would need some sort of intense therapy and started looking into things like dialectical behavior therapy, but never signed up.

Then, in January 2019, my dad messaged me on Facebook and told me about the "Iceman" and Wim Hof Method that he had learned about from a Joe Rogan podcast. My dad and I have always been very much into researching holistic mental health remedies, so I was naturally very intrigued. I was consumed in researching the method, and from the time I did my first breathing exercises, I was hooked! I did the breathing and ended my showers with cold water religiously for two weeks. Then...I stopped. I got sick, and it was hard to do the breath work without a coughing attack. I got through the sickness, but I didn't start back up again, and then my mental health tanked. During those first two weeks of practicing the WHM, I felt great. No lows, or "storms," just a steady contentment. But when I stopped, I spiraled downward into a mild depression. My husband realized just how much I needed to practice WHM consistently, so he became my biggest supporter.

Since February 2019, I have not missed a day of practicing, I've completed the Fundamentals course, I have attended weekend workshops with amazing WHM instructors, Jesse Coomer, James Stewart, and Jarad Blantonand, and have just returned from the Poland expedition with Wim Hof himself! So many people had breakthroughs and realizations. We shared hundreds of hugs over the course of five days, along with tears, laughter, dancing (his nickname for me is Dancer of Life, one-hour-plus-long breath sessions, waterfall swims, and, of course, that powerful force of simple human connection and love. Wim was his kind, musical, goofy, and relentless self, whose goal is to help people be the happiest they can be by pushing out of their comfort zone and going within. It was an honor to ascend the mountain alongside him and all of the other beautiful souls!

The WHM has completely changed my life. I have not experienced a full-blown RSD episode or any sort of prolonged mild depression, and because of that, my marriage, work life, friendships, family relationships, and overall sense of well-being have improved beyond anything I thought possible with something as simple as cold exposure, mindset, and breathing exercises! I am grateful every day, and my wish is for everyone to be able to utilize lifestyle changes to optimize their health, and I truly believe incorporating the Wim Hof Method into a

daily routine is one of the best ways to do so!"
~ Jessica Johnson (Dancer of Life)

Dan contracted whooping cough from his son in 2014 after dealing with the stress of his wife's recent cancer diagnosis. Over the next few months, as a result of the whooping cough and a weakened immune system from all the stress, Dan's condition worsened. When he finally went to the doctor, he discovered he had an autoimmune disorder called Guillain-Barre, which eats the myelin sheath off the nerves and mimics symptoms of multiple sclerosis, which rendered him completely paralyzed. His diagnosis was a 50 percent chance of permanent paralysis, and the recovery would take eighteen to twenty-four months. There is no cure. Still partially paralyzed, he was sent home after a month.

Four months later, Dan's son suggested he try the WHM after hearing about Wim Hof and his superhuman strength and immune system. Dan immediately bought the ten-week Fundamentals Course and began incorporating the practices into his daily recovery. Eight months later, he was completely symptom-free, and he remains so. He is the strongest and healthiest he has ever been. At age sixty-four, Dan swims two miles in the ocean three times a week, deadlifts 300 pounds, can do the splits, has no inflammation in his body, and has more energy than he ever has. "You really need to stimulate and stress your autonomic nervous system to be healthy," says Dan.[119]

Eric suffered a catastrophic injury while on active duty as a Marine Corps officer years ago. Falling from a rope, Eric jammed his left leg into his hip socket, tore the cartilage in his left hip, dislocated his pelvis, crushed two bottom discs in his spine, and contorted two other discs in his neck. For years, he tried to manage the pain with a number of pain-killing medications while dealing with the accumulating mental toll from his work, which involved composing and delivering letters to the families of soldiers who had passed away. This manifested in depression, anxiety, and addiction.

Eric then learned of the WHM. "When I started doing the ice baths, and when I started doing the breathing, I started tapering myself off of medication, and now I no longer take anything for pain other than just breathing and taking daily ice baths," says Eric. "By far the best takeaway from the Wim Hof Method was the cognitive or mental benefit. The ice bath is a wonderful training tool. It affords you the opportunity to go into that stressful situation. You're training your mind and rewiring your brain to then learn how to relax, de-stress, or be stronger in any other possible situation. Once I learned how to do that, life got exponentially easier."[120]

A violin player and mother of five, Sophie has suffered with multiple sclerosis for years. As a result, she could not use the left side of her body and therefore could no longer play violin; it became much too difficult. After starting the WHM, she noticed a tingling sensation in her fingers when she would do the breathing exercises. She was shocked, as she was certain she would never feel anything in her fingers again. Even her doctor told her to stop playing piano, telling her, "It's a lost cause. I hope you can accept that."

Now that she's practicing the WHM, Sophie says, "everyday it feels like I am resetting my body because of the breathing exercises and the cold shower. I can really feel something is happening. With the breathing, it's like I'm turning my body on. And with the shower, it's like I'm preparing my body's army to temper, or withstand, any attacks from this disease. If I don't practice it for one day, which actually doesn't really happen, at first it bothers me mentally, it doesn't feel right, and after a while it translates into my physical well- being. I don't use any medicine. I practice the Wim Hof Method." The WHM is "like a daily injection that I should have injected in my leg, according to my neurologist. It has been a way of life for me, absolutely. I can see myself doing this for the rest of my life. I don't have any doubts about that. I'm totally living the life I want to live. I help out at my kids' school. I take them to school. I pick them up. It wasn't always like that. There is a constant energy flow that I'm getting, and that's a really big difference. My MS doesn't need to be reckoned with. I can do what I want."[121]

Nutritionist Josh says, "If you can positively influence the body's ability to receive oxygen, you single handedly, positively influence every system of the body. You naturally then change the chemistry of your brain, endocrine system, and also influence dramatically the acidification that's going on in the body, improving the alkalinity. And why is that important? Because that is the governing system of the body. If you're acidified through diet, water, air, EMF's, all of these things in the modern-day world are very acidic. We have to get back to the core of our health. And oxygen is the spark of every single healthy cell in the body. So, without it, you can take anything you want, you can take any magic pill, or anything, and you'll never get to the correct operating system of the body, and that's by oxygen." Josh thinks the Wim Hof Method is "the most powerful thing you can do to do the most primary thing you can for your health. And that's increasing red blood cells, oxygen, and decreasing acidification in the body. By positively affecting the PH of your body, the red blood cells of your body by your diet, you're amplifying your body's ability to receive oxygen. If you create a body that's alkaline, eating fresh fruits and vegetables, then you're allowing, and creating an environment so that when you breathe in, your body can receive more of that oxygen. So, the intersection between proper nutrition and taking in that oxygen, is essential for optimal health."[122]

Luuk lives in Blaricum, Holland, where he runs a forge. In 1984, he was diagnosed with rheumatism, and despite the difficulty, Luuk continued working but had to get surgery on his fingers and elbow. His shoulders, knee, and wrist were affected and worsened to the point where he could barely walk. He took pain medications until one of them stopped working. A family friend recommended Luuk pay Wim Hof, who lived nearby, a visit. At first, Luuk wanted nothing to do with the cold water. "I'm not going into the cold. No way," he said. During his visit, Hof challenged Luuk to try out the ice bath plus some breathing techniques, as well as thirty push-ups, which Luuk thought was impossible, as he could barely walk.

"No thanks," said Luuk, "I'm going home."

"What's your name?" Hof replied.

"Luuk."

"You're going to do forty push-ups," exclaimed Hof.

The next morning, Luuk paid Hof a second visit, and they began with forty-five minutes of Hof's breathing technique, and then Luuk managed to do the forty push-ups Hof promised him.

Luuk was shocked. "I gave it everything and somehow succeeded. With that push-ups exercise, he really showed me what my body was capable of," he said. "So, I started taking cold showers, which I really hated at first. I really didn't like it. Just getting one leg underwater… Jesus Lord. You're thinking, shit, I don't want this. But I also thought, If he can do it, then why can't I? Despite his rheumatologist's warnings, Luuk decided to give the WHM a try. His blood levels soon started improving, and his infection values decreased. He became more fit, stronger, and healthier, and before he knew it, his rheumatism had been "neutralized for the most part."

"I'm not saying the rheumatism has gone up in smoke, but it has come to a halt," said Luuk. "I don't want to state that the Wim Hof Method is the answer to rheumatism, yet adopting the Wim Hof Method requires a change in lifestyle, and that certainly triggers stuff in your body. It has impacted my life in such a way that it has increased my performance. ... I also want to stress that it's not only the Wim Hof Method that has helped me. But it's an important part of the whole spectrum. You also become more aware of what you eat. You become more active, practice yoga more, and focus on your mindset. It's a matter of trying out new stuff to get your health back in shape. I also want to make clear that this whole endeavor is for life. I'm going to stick with it. I enjoy practicing the method. And I hope to enthuse other people to try it, too. But you have to really want it. Don't even bother if you don't want it. Go read the newspaper or watch a movie, don't bother trying it. But if you feel compelled to give it a go, and you can really believe you can change, then you should go for it. And fully commit to it for months. And then see what happens."[123]

Alistair Overeem has been training as a professional fighter for twenty-two years, competing in the Ultimate Fighting Championship for nineteen of those years. "I'd heard several stories about him [Wim] from friends, and I became curious," he said. "As an athlete, I'm always looking to gain that edge, to gain an advantage over my opponents, and his breathing techniques and withstanding the cold intrigued me, especially the breathing techniques. Everybody needs oxygen, and as an athlete, you cannot have enough oxygen. Breathing is a very big component."

Alistair started training with Wim for his upcoming shot at the UFC Championship. He incorporated the breathing techniques and ice baths into his training regimen. Being half Jamaican, he was not excited about the cold, but he conquered it to improve his performance. After the fight, Alistair said, "I felt the nerves coming, but I just reverted back to the breathing exercises that I had been practicing daily, and I was very calm. Very calm on fight day, very calm during the whole day, during the whole process. Of course, you feel a little tension, but every time I felt that tension, I just went back to the breathing, and I was calm, and I felt energetic. During the fight, I was breathing correctly." On December 19, 2015, Alistair took the title from Junior Dos Santos by knockout in the last seconds of the second round. "Usually, a fight is three rounds," says Alistair, but "I also wasn't tired. So, for my cardio, it really increased, just by breathing, breathing correctly."

He adds, "I am definitely recommending it to everybody! It is a truly unique method. It's a unique method that's going to change the world."[124]

World-renowned big wave surfer Laird Hamilton has been an advocate of the WHM for many years. "I have always been in search of different techniques to improve performance and ultimately make me a better person. I came across the 'Iceman,' and I was really intrigued by his work, and it led me to Mr. Wim Hof himself and his method," says Laird. "I was able to go online and get a course. There's not a person alive who can't benefit from it. I did the course, and I continue to do the course. The implications of doing this are immense. Not only does it bring a calmness to your spirit, which is probably the most important thing, but it's enhanced my performance, and I believe this is a tool that I'll be able to use in the future to combat sickness and disease and any other thing that I have to deal with in my life. I'm very grateful for Wim's work, and I continue to be a warrior for his cause."[125]

Stoic Philosophy

The following testimonials are from a Facebook group called "Stoicism."

"Before I was diagnosed at age fifty-three with bipolar disorder, I had attempted to take my life three times over the years. I believe it was my constant pursuit of peace that led me to accidentally discover this way of living, even before all the medicine I take for it now. I learned to do what I called 'projects,' that basically involved intentionally living out one of the cardinal, or ordinal, virtues at a time. Sound familiar? So, in a way, I was practicing the Stoic way of living before I knew what it was. Cognitive behavioral therapy also taught me that perspective shapes our thoughts, which are merely opinions. That gave me the empathy to connect with people through the 'greater mind.' I now understand how this way of living is the Stoic way. My purpose for studying this philosophy is to learn how to live for the pursuit of virtue and to be in love with life. I am a disabled veteran because of the severity of my condition. I am such a happy guy now, never depressed! But I still get occasional mania and addictive behavior that I mix up with being satisfied with my life. When I wake up in the morning, I commit myself to a virtue. It doesn't matter what happened yesterday, my emotions, or opinions about it, no matter how intense. After nearly seventy years of experience, and my new Stoic understanding, I choose, over all the noise, to stay true to this choice. I am really inspired by the hope that this way of living provides, along with the other solutions I have come up with, including my combination of medicine. That took years to discover."

~ James

"I faced severe depression years ago. I tried everything

to solve it without medication. I worked out, ate healthier, spent time with friends, cut back on stress, and more. Stoicism made sense to me when I found it in high school. It was exactly what I needed, but it would only help me for a few more years before it was no longer enough. Then, I started taking medication for about six months. This allowed my brain to reset at a calmer level. During this time, I introduced Stoicism into the framework of my brain and my thoughts. My thinking was that if I can hardwire myself to be this way while the medication is allowing me to relax, I can create a new baseline and not need medication anymore. Here I am today, a lot happier, and medication-free! Not everyone will be able to get off of their medications, but Stoicism can help find a new baseline. I also use Stoicism in my care of psychiatric patients to teach them better coping skills with life that they may have never needed to have before recent life events brought them to the hospital, whether it was a divorce, death of a loved one, or other meaningful losses."

~ Malkan

RESOURCES

TAKING BACK MY MIND

Website: takingbackmymind.com

Blog: takingbackmymind.com/blog

Podcasts: takingbackmymind.com/podcasts

Events: takingbackmymind.com/events

Merchandise: takingbackmymind.com/shop

BOOKS

Inspiration and Advice

The Power of Now by Eckhart Tolle
   In the present moment lies your freedom, Tolle writes. It really does.

Letting Go: The Pathway of Surrender by David R. Hawkins

The Four Agreements by Don Miguel Ruiz
   Follow these tenets and you will never have a problem:
   1. Be impeccable with your word.
   2. Don't take anything personally.
   3. Don't make assumptions.
   4. Always do your best.

The Body Keeps the Score: Brain, Mind, and Body in the Healing of Trauma by Bessel Van der Kolk

Alexander McFarlane, director of the Centre for Traumatic Stress Studies, calls this book "essential reading for anyone interested in understanding and treating traumatic stress and the scope of its impact on society."

Waking the Tiger: Healing Trauma by Peter A. Levine

A new and hopeful vision of trauma, this book views the human animal as a unique being, endowed with an instinctual capacity. It asks and answers an intriguing question: Why are animals in the wild, though threatened routinely, rarely traumatized? By understanding the dynamics that make wild animals virtually immune to traumatic symptoms, the mystery of human trauma is revealed.

The Biology of Belief by Dr. Bruce H. Lipton, Ph.D.

Dr. Bruce Lipton has received widespread acclaim as one of the most accessible and knowledgeable voices of "new biology." Sparking the study of epigenetics, a revolutionary field that shows us how the energy of consciousness is as important in shaping life on earth as DNA and chemistry, in the 1970s, Lipton brings clarity, insight, and humor to unveiling a profound change in how we perceive the way life works. As scientists have mapped the human genome, it has become clear there are important aspects of life that defy our traditional models of evolution. The "missing link," according to Lipton, is consciousness.

Becoming Supernatural: How Common People are Doing the Uncommon by Dr. Joe Dizpenza

Dr. Joe Dispenza explains how humans are quite literally supernatural by nature if given the proper knowledge and instruction and how, by applying that information through various meditations, we can experience a greater expression of our creative abilities. Dispenza explains our capacity to tune in to frequencies beyond our material world and receive more orderly coherent streams of consciousness and energy, how we can intentionally change our brain chemistry to initiate profoundly mystical transcendental experiences, and how we can develop the skill of creating a more efficient, balanced, healthy body, a more unlimited mind, and greater access to the realms of spiritual truth.

When the Body Says No: The Cost of Hidden Stress by Dr. Gabor Maté

Drawing on deep scientific research and Dr. Gabor Maté's acclaimed clinical work, this book provides answers to critical questions about the mind-body link and the role stress and our emotional makeup play in an array of common diseases such as arthritis, cancer, diabetes, heart disease, irritable bowel syndrome, and multiple sclerosis. With dozens of case studies and stories, including those of Lou Gehrig, Betty Ford, and Lance Armstrong, Maté reveals the principles for healing and prevention of illness from hidden stress.

Psychedelics

How to Change Your Mind: What the New Science of Psychedelics Teaches Us About Consciousness, Dying, Addiction, Depression, and Transcendence by Michael Pollan

Consciousness Medicine: Indigenous Wisdom, Entheogens, and Expanded States of Consciousness for Healing by Françoise Bourzat

A Really Good Day: How Microdosing Made a Mega Difference in My Mood, My Marriage, and My Life by Ayelet Waldman

The Doors of Perception by Aldous Huxley

The Psychedelic Explorer's Guide: Safe, Therapeutic, and Sacred Journeys by James Fadiman

Wim Hof Method

The Wim Hof Method: Activate Your Full Human Potential by Wim Hof
The only definitive book by Wim Hof on his powerful method for realizing our physical and spiritual potential.

Becoming the Iceman by Wim Hof and Justin Rosales
Wim Hof and Justin Rosales show the world that anyone can become an Iceman or Icewoman, that the ability to control the body's temperature is not a genetic defect in Wim.

What Doesn't Kill Us: How Freezing Water, Extreme Altitude, and Environmental Conditioning Will Renew Our Lost Evolutionary Strength by Scott Carney
Can we hack our bodies and use the environment to stimulate our inner biology? Investigative journalist and anthropologist Scott Carney takes up the challenge to find out. Helping him in his search are Wim Hof, an Army scientist, a world-famous surfer, the founders of an obstacle course race movement, and ordinary people who have documented how they have cured autoimmune diseases, lost weight, and reversed diabetes. Carney chronicles his own transformational journey as he pushes his body and mind to the edge of endurance, a quest that culminates in a record-bending, 28-hour climb to the snowy peak of Mt. Kilimanjaro wearing nothing but a pair of running shorts and sneakers.

The Way of The Iceman: How The Wim Hof Method Creates Radiant Longterm Health: Using The Science and Secrets of Breath Control, Cold-Training, and Commitment by Wim Hof and Koen De Jong

Stoic Philosophy

The Daily Stoic: Stoic Wisdom for Everyday Life by Ryan Holiday

The Five Minute Journal: A Happier You in 5 Minutes a Day

Meditations by Marcus Aurelius
A series of the Roman emporer's personal writings from 161 to 180 AD, recording his private notes to himself and ideas on Stoic philosophy. Aurelius wrote the meditations as a source for his own guidance and self-improvement.

Letters from a Stoic by Seneca
A masterpiece of classical literature, this book offers a compelling and accessible introduction to Stoic ideas, which Seneca uses to offer practical advice on a number of real-world problems, as relevant today as it was then.

The Enchiridion by Epictetus
The *Enchiridion,* or "handbook," is a short manual of Stoic ethical advice.

Discourses by Epictetus
A series of informal lectures by the Stoic philosopher.

The Little Book of Stoicism: Timeless Wisdom to Gain Resilience, Confidence, and Calmness by Jonas Salzgeber

The Obstacle is the Way: The Timeless Art of Turning Trials into

Triumph by Ryan Holiday

Ego is the Enemy by Ryan Holiday

The Daily Stoic: 366 Meditations on Wisdom, Perseverance, and the Art of Living by Ryan Holiday and Stephen Hanselman

How to think like a Roman Emperor: The Stoic Philosophy of Marcus Aurelius by Donald Robertson

The Subtle Art of Not Giving a Fuck: A Counterintuitive Approach to Living a Good Life by Mark Manson

RESEARCH INSTITUTES AND PSYCHEDELIC HEALING

Multidisciplinary Association for Psychedelic Studies (MAPS)
Founded in 1986, MAPS is a non-profit research and educational organization that develops medical, legal, and cultural contexts for people to benefit from the careful uses of psychedelics and cannabis. maps.org

Johns Hopkins: Center for Psychedelic & Consciousness Research
hopkinspsychedelic.org

Imperial College, London: Centre for Psychedelic Research
imperial.ac.uk/psychedelic-research-centre

San Francisco Psychedelic Society
psychedelicsocietysf.org

Psychedelic Insights
Facilitates consciousness expansion and inner peace through psychedelic-assisted psychotherapy. psychedelicinsights.com

Fireside Project
Psychedelic peer-support line providing live support via phone or text for people on a journey, trip sitting, or in need of guidance with post-journey integration. 6-2FIRESIDE (623-473-7433), available only in the United States. firesideproject.org

ACKNOWLEDGMENTS

I never thought about being an author, let alone an author about my tragedies in 2017. Had anyone told me this before December 22, 2017, I would have told them they were absolutely nuts. Yet here I am in the final edit of my first book, and as I type these words, we are in the midst of the 2020 lockdown as the world is changing in ways we can't yet imagine. At first, I thought, great... another obstacle, what bad timing. But then I realized there is no time more fitting for the subjects of this book: how to cultivate resilience, fortitude, and strength, how to weather the storms of life. This is quite a hurricane that has swept the world over. The timing couldn't be better.

It has been a magical, educational, enlightening, and beautiful journey, to say the least. When I first thought about writing this book, I had no idea where to start. I had started journaling days after my mind was liberated from its suffering, so I figured I could just compile my notes and hope it would develop into a story somehow. The pieces started slowly falling into place, the story started taking shape, and over time the vision became more clear. This vision seemed to download into my mind during my meditations (especially during heavy Wim Hof sessions), morning yoga routines, and several psychedelic journeys, each time solidifying the goal: to help those who are suffering as I was. I discovered the power of visualization. Nearly every step of the way, the things I have visualized have come to fruition and manifested in the most amazing, coincidental ways.

This also has been the most challenging journey I have ever embarked on. I made several failed attempts to find a publisher and my Kickstarter campaign to fund the book's printing failed. So, I am self-publishing. I have learned so much about myself and the world around me, and I am so very grateful for the knowledge I have learned over the course of this journey, knowledge I depended on to overcome the many difficult moments, continual challenges, emotional roller coasters, and countless obstacles. I am forever grateful for the teachers from whom I have learned who are found throughout this book and for all the scientists, researchers, writers, health practitioners, and philosophers whose work has been an integral part of it. A special thank you to Wim Hof; my life would not be the same without the Wim Hof Method. Thank you all for your wisdom.

None of this would have been possible, and it is questionable if I would even be alive if it weren't for my brother, who took that fateful walk on the beach with me that beautiful December day in 2017. Thank you, bro, you saved my life. Nor would this have been possible without the unconditional love, acceptance, and understanding of my sister, who took me in on her couch for those ten months I was destroying myself. She fed me, provided for me, and never hesitated to help me in any way that she could. Thank you, Rosa. Nor would I be where I am if it weren't for the several conversations I had with Noam—a complete stranger whom I have not even met in person yet—who talked me off the ledge so many times and asked for nothing in return.. Thank you, Noam, you seriously helped save my life in such a big way. You were so right about everything; I no longer identify with the depression that almost killed me. I am astounded at your wisdom. I would like to thank my sister Lilia and my brother Leo for spending countless hours helping me edit the ever-evolving manuscript when it was in its first stages, as well as the rest of my family for caring and showing support however they could. I owe an honorary mention to my good friend and amazing yoga instructor, Anna Zehringer, for helping me research and write the yoga and meditation chapter. A very special thank you to my good friends Kim and Donna Butler for helping me format the paperback manuscript when I had no idea what I was doing. Thank you! I also owe a very special thank you to my editor Robyn Lawrence for her amazing editing skills and for completely revamping the book and really taking it up a notch. Thank you SO much! If this book ever makes the New York Times Best Seller list, it will be because of you! I would like to thank my lifelong friends Mike and Mark, who have become brothers to me, and the entire Regalado family for being like a second family to me and a big part of my story. Thank you all for the great times. It's been a hell of a ride!

A special thank you to Safe Spaces Amsterdam and Psychedelic Insights for providing their patients' testimonials as well as Nicole Amelia, Shawn Cameron, Andreas Gustafsson, Jessica Johnson, Malkan [last name omitted by request], and James [last name omitted by request], for their personal testimonies, and Mike Tyson, Doug Steiny, Brad Carson, Anuschka Franken, Daren Olien, Henk Van Den Bergh, Alistair Overeem, Laird Hamilton, Tim Ferriss, and James Bond Stockdale, whom I mention in this book, for being such powerful guiding lights, and of course, Michael Pollan and the entire psychedelic community for all their hard work and research upon which much of the book's content is based.

Lastly, I owe a debt of gratitude to the ancient Stoics, especially Marcus Aurelius, Seneca, and Epictetus for their timeless wisdom.

Throughout this journey, there have been supporters and non-supporters, believers and non-believers. There have been people who have lifted me up, encouraged me, and believed in me, and there have been naysayers. I would like to thank them all because, while hard to see sometimes, even the naysayers have a priceless quality that goes unnoticed to the untrained eye. Those who challenge us and make life difficult for us are simply the means for us to question our own assumptions, to learn to control our emotions, and to face our own demons. They offer us an opportunity to grow.

In every challenge encountered, in every difficult situation, there is a valuable lesson to learn. Everyone plays a part in this life, and I am forever grateful for every actor in this play and feel so lucky for my role in it. Thank you all for your role.

ABOUT THE AUTHOR

Gerardo Urias splits his time between Mexico and his hometown of San Diego, California, where he continues working to raise awareness about alternative therapies for mental, emotional, spiritual, and physical health. Through doing so, Gerardo wishes to help others reach their full potential, which he believes is the first step to contributing to positive world change. His vision is to help advance psychedelic research and create wellness retreats consisting of the practices he writes about around the world. When Gerardo is not writing, he is surfing, skiing, rock climbing, traveling, spending time with friends and family, and reading.

Learn more about Gerardo's projects at www.takingbackmymind.com/events.

END NOTES

[1] Michael Pollan. *How To Change Your Mind: What the New Science of Psychedelics Teaches Us About Consciousness, Dying, Addiction, Depression, and Transcendence* (New York: Penguin Press, 2018): 212, Kindle.

[2] eurekalert.org/pub_releases/2021-03/ss-nr032921.php.

[3] drugscience.org.uk/.

[4] mindmedicineaustralia.org.au/

[5] maps.org/research/mdma/ptsd/phase3.

[6] Pollan (2018): 166.

[7] Ibid., 163.

[8] Ibid., 30.

[9] Pollan (2018): 71.

[10] Stephen Kinzer. *Poisoner In Chief: Sidney Gottlieb and the CIA Search for Mind Control*, (New York: Henry Holt & Company, 2019).

[11] Mike Jay. The Acid Farmers, 2018. mikejay.net/the-acid-farmers

[12] Pollan (2018): 7.

[13] Pollan (2018): 132.

[14] Linda Greenhouse. Sect Allowed to Import Its Hallucinogenic Tea, *The New York Times*, (February 22, 2006).

[15] Michael P Bogenschutz, Alyssa A Forcehimes, Jessica A Pommy, Claire E Wilcox, PCR Barbosa, Rick J Strassman. Psilocybin-Assisted Treatment for Alcohol Dependence: A Proof-of-concept Study. *Journal of Psychopharmacology* 29, no. 3 (2015): 289-99. doi: 10.1177/0269881114565144

[16] Matthew W Johnson, Albert Garcia-Romeu, Roland R Griffiths. Long-term Follow-up of Psilocybin-facilitated Smoking Cessation. *The*

American Journal of Drug and Alcohol Abuse 43, no.1 (2017): 55-60. doi: 10.3109/00952990.2016.1170135

[17] Grant Jones, Joceyln A. Ricard, Joshua Lipson, Matthew K. Nock, Associations Between Classic Psychedelics and Opioid-Use Disorder in a Nationally Representative U.S. Adult Sample. *Scientific Reports* 12, 4099 (2022). 'doi.org/10.1038/s41598-022-08085-4

[18] Katherine A MacLean, Matthew W Johnson, Roland R Griffiths. Mystical Experiences Occasioned by the Hallucinogen Psilocybin Lead to Increases in the Personality Domain of Openness. *Journal of Psychopharmacology* 25, no. 11 (2011): 1453-1461. doi: 10.1177/026988111142018.

[19] Pollan (2018): 54.

[20] Roland R Griffiths, Matthew W Johnson, Michael A Carducci, Annie Umbricht, William A Richards, Brian D Richards, Mary P Cosimano, Margaret A Klinedinst. Psilocybin Produces Substantial and Sustained Decreases in Depression and Anxiety in Patients with Life-Threatening Cancer: A Randomized Double-Blind Trial. *Journal of Psychopharmacology* 30, no. 12 (2016): 1181–97. doi: 10.1177/0269881116675513

[21] R.E. Daws, C. Timmermann, B. Giribaldi, *et al.* Increased global integration in the brain after psilocybin therapy for depression. *Nat Med* 28, 844–851 (2022). doi.org/10.1038/s41591-022-01744-z

[22] Kai Kupferschmidt. "All Clear for the Decisive Trial of Ecstasy in PTSD Patients," *Science Magazine,* August 26, 2017. doi: 10.1126/science.aap7739

[23] Ibid., 334.

[24] Philip Jaekl. Turns out Near-death Experiences are Psychedelic, not Religious," Wired: *Neuroscience*, August 15, 2018. wired.co.uk/article/near-death-experiences-psychedelic-religious

[25] Pollan (2018): 345.

[26] Pollan (2018): 358.

[27] Ibid., 352.

[28] Greta Thunberg. School Strike for Climate - Save the World by

Changing the Rules, December 12, 2018, *TedX*: Stokholm, Sweden, video, 11:10, www.youtube.com/watch?v=EAmmUIEsN9A

[29] Xavier Francuski, "Can Psychedelics Induce Flow States," The Third Wave, June 14, 2018, https://thethirdwave.co/psychedelics-flow/

[30] Steven Kotler. "The Science of Peak Human Performance," *Time*, April 30, 2014, Accessed May 30, 2022. https://time.com/56809/the-science-of-peak-human-performance/.

[31] Csikszentmihalyi, Mihaly (1990). Flow: The Psychology of Optimal Experience. New York, NY: Harper and Row.

[32] Charles J. Limb, Allen R. Braun, "Neural Substrates of Spontaneous Musical Performance: An fMRI Study of Jazz Improvisation," *PLOS One* 3, no. 2 (2008): e1679. Doi: 10.1371/journal.pone.0001679.

[33] Robin L Carhart-Harris, Robert Leech, Peter J Hellyer, Murray Shanahan, Amanda Feilding, Enzo Tagliazucchi, Dante R Chialvo, David Nutt. The Entropic Brain: a Theory of Conscious States Informed by Neuroimaging Research with Psychedelic Drugs." *Frontiers in Human Neuroscience* 8, no. 20 (2014). doi: 10.3389/fnhum.2014.00020

[34] Ibid, 357.

[35] Ibid, 359.

[36] Ibid, 348.

[37] "Denver Election Results, 2019," *The Denver Post*, May 7, 2019. https://www.denverpost.com/2019/05/07/denver-election-results-2019/

[38] Jaeger, Kyle, "City Council Unanimously Votes To Decriminalize Psychedelics In Ann Arbor, Michigan," September 22, 2020, Marijuana Moment. Accessed April 11, 2021.
https://www.marijuanamoment.net/city-council-unanimously-votes-to-decriminalize-psychedelics-in-ann-arbor-michigan/

[39] Feuer, Will, "Oregon becomes first state to legalize magic mushrooms as more states ease drug laws in 'psychedelic renaissance,'" November 4, 2020, CNBC. Accessed April 11, 2021. https://www.cnbc.com/2020/11/04/oregon-becomes-first-state-to-legalize-magic-mushrooms-as-more-states-ease-drug-laws.html

[40] Matt Pusatory, "Magic mushrooms officially decriminalized in DC," WUSA9. March 16, 2021. Accessed April 11, 2021. https://www.wusa9.com/article/news/local/dc/dc-magic-mushroom-decriminalized-as-of-march-16/65-d7d47bdc-60f4-497d-81e9-e9db4d109406.

[41] Jerilyn Jordan, "Washtenaw County says cases involving natural psychedelics will no longer be charged."January 12, 2021. Detroit Metro Times. Accessed April 11, 2021. https://www.metrotimes.com/detroit/washtenaw-county-prosecutor-announces-cases-involving-marijuana-magic-mushrooms-and-psychedelic-plants-will-no-longer-be-charged/Content?oid=26218702.

[42] Margolin, Madison, "Breaking: Somerville, Massachusetts Votes to "Decriminalize Nature". DoubleBlind Mag. March 12, 2021. Retrieved April 11, 2021. https://doubleblindmag.com/somerville-massachusetts-decriminalize-nature/

[43] Levy, Marc, "War on use of mushrooms, cacti and ayahuasca has been called off in Cambridge by council order," February 4, 2021, Cambridge Day. Accessed April 11, 2021. https://www.cambridgeday.com/2021/02/04/war-on-use-of-mushrooms-cacti-and-ayahuasca-has-been-called-off-in-cambridge-by-council-order/

[44] Esther Honig, "A Growing Push To Loosen Laws Around Psilocybin, Treat Mushrooms As Medicine," May 7, 2019, NPR. Accessed April 11, 2021. https://www.npr.org/sections/health-shots/2019/05/07/720828367/a-growing-push-to-loosen-laws-around-psilocybin-treat-mushrooms-as-medicine.

[45] Dom Amato, "Should Vermont decriminalize some hallucinogenic drugs?" WCAX-TV. January 23, 2020. Retrieved April 11, 2021. https://www.wcax.com/content/news/Should-Vermont-decriminalize-some-hallucinogenic-drugs-567241491.html

[46] Newsfile Corp, May 5, 2020, "This is Why Lawmakers are Pushing to Decriminalize Psychedelic Mushrooms." Yahoo! Finance. Accessed April 11, 2021. https://finance.yahoo.com/news/why-lawmakers-pushing-decriminalize-psychedelic-

120700426.html?guccounter=1&guce_referrer=aHR0cHM6Ly9lbi53a
WtpcGVkaWEub3JnLw&guce_referrer_sig=AQAAABvoGh-
EHtd7AelWdNSxINInghKNQCyMA6AqohYJ9gUnZG0zMBCFYDN
AXWUH8VW3fP6NfPEciuGmbiOWw9If742xmVVeHwZw8TR7PfE
XfqXaoEtqqiaWQ_ulxyoINZwEqQDS7nSVuy8Clis1Fr-XThQ-w2-
idAZRVpoOVkicy9kI.

[47] Amanda Hoover, NJ Advance Media For NJ. com, November 17, 2020. "Marijuana decriminalization stalls in N.J. Assembly after lawmakers add magic mushrooms to the bill. Senate moves forward". nj. Retrieved April 11, 2021. https://www.nj.com/marijuana/2020/11/marijuana-decriminalization-stalls-in-nj-assembly-after-lawmakers-add-magic-mushrooms-to-the-bill.html.

[48] Lozano, Alicia Victoria, "New California bill would decriminalize psychedelics, expunge criminal records," February 18, 2021. NBC News. Accessed April 11, 2021. https://www.nbcnews.com/news/us-news/new-california-bill-would-decriminalize-psychedelics-expunge-criminal-records-n1258261.

[49] Kyle Jaeger, "Nearly 100 Cities Are Considering Decriminalizing Psychedelics, Map Shows," *Marijuana Moment: Politics*, November 29, 2019. Accessed April 11, 2019. https://www.marijuanamoment.net/nearly-100-cities-are-considering-decriminalizing-psychedelics-map-shows/?fbclid=IwAR0MwtCfHbY7eWLaCa7ol-ADba_TptrPrt1urdD1upMUn6E9cprxctNVQ_c.

[50] NA White Booklet, *Narcotics Anonymous*, 1976.

[51] Epictetus, *Discourses*.

[52] AA Fact File, Birth of AA. http://www.aa.org/assets/en_US/m-24_aafactfile.pdf

[53] Pollan (2018): 176.

[54] *Pass it on: The Story of Bill Wilson and How the A.A. Message Reached the World* (New York: Alcoholics Anonymous World Services, 1984).

[55] Keith Humphreys, Janet C Blodgett, Todd H Wagner. "Estimating

the Efficacy of Alcoholics Anonymous without Self-Selection Bias: An Instrumental Variables Re-Analysis of Randomized Clinical Trials," *Alcoholism: Clinical & Experimental Research* 38, no. 11 (2014). doi: 10.1111/acer.12557

[56] Katie Hunt. A Woman Took 550 Times the Usual Dose of LSD, with Surprisingly Positive Consequences, *CNN*: Health, March 1, 2020, https://edition.cnn.com/2020/02/27/health/lsd-overdoses-case-studies-wellness/index.html?fbclid= IwAR1XnXj0J5DJ0xYYg8pFXUM_1_LZNBaxt-ncymf1lBQyJ2qQTrgNZghhQG8

[57] Centers for Disease Control and Prevention (CDC). Alcohol Use and Your Health, *CDC*: Alcohol and Public Health. https://www.cdc.gov/alcohol/fact-sheets/alcohol-use.htm (Accessed November 20, 2019)

[58] Mandy Stahre, Jim Roeber, Dafna Kanny, Robert D Brewer, Xingyou Zhang. Contribution of Excessive Alcohol Consumption to Deaths and Years of Potential Life Lost in the United States. *Prev Chronic Dis* 11: 130293 (2014). doi: 10.5888/pcd11.130293

[59] Lizmarie Maldonado. Alcoholism Statistics and Important Facts, *Project Know: Drug Addiction Statistics*. https://www.projectknow.com/drug-addiction/statistics/ (Accessed November 22, 2019)

[60] Jun Wang, Yifeng Cheng, Xuehua Wang, Emily Roltsch Hellard, Tengfei Ma, Hannah Gil, Sami Ben Hamida and Dorit Ron. Alcohol Elicits Functional and Structural Plasticity Selectively in Dopamine D1 Receptor-Expressing Neurons of the Dorsomedial Striatum, *Journal of Neuroscience* 35, no. 33 (2015): 11634 - 11643. doi: 10.1523/JNEUROSCI.0003-15.2015

[61] Johann Hari. Everything You Think You Know About Addiction is Wrong, *Ted Talks*, London, England, Youtube, June 2015. https://www.youtube.com/watch?v=PY9DcIMGxMs&t=576s

[62] Glen Greenwald. Drug Decriminalization in Portugal: Lessons for Creating Fair and Successful Drug Policies, *Cato Institute Whitepaper Series*, April 2, 2009. doi: 10.2139/ssrn.1464837

[63] Vice Documentary, Inside the Superhuman World of Wim Hof: The Iceman, *YouTube*, July 16, 2015. https://www.youtube.com/watch?time_continue=8&v=VaMjhwFE1Zw

[64] Wikipedia, *Wim Hof: Personal Life*. https://en.wikipedia.org/wiki/Wim_Hof (accessed February 13, 2020).

[65] Dutch Iceman to Climb Everest in Shorts: It's all about the Inner Fire," *ExplorersWeb*, March 1, 2007, accessed February 13, 2020. https://www.explorersweb.com/everest_k2/news.php?id=15688

[66] Kathmandu, Everest Climber Falls Short, *The Age*, May 29, 2007, accessed February 13, 2020. https://www.theage.com.au/world/everest-climber-falls-short-20070529-ge504f.html

[67] Craig Mackenzie. Burning Man: Adventurer Loses 14lbs as he Completes Marathon in 40C Namibia Without Touching a Drop of Water, *Daily Mail*, December 9, 2011.
https://www.dailymail.co.uk/news/article-2072156/Burning-man-Adventurer-loses-14lbs-completes-marathon-40C-Nambia-touching-drop-water.html

[68] Radboud University Nijmegen Medical Centre. Research on 'Iceman' Wim Hof Suggests it May be Possible to Influence Autonomic Nervous System and Immune Response. *ScienceDaily*.
www.sciencedaily.com/releases/2011/04/110422090203.htm (accessed February 13, 2020)

[69] Matthijs Kox, Lucas T van Eijk, Jelle Zwaag, Joanne van den Wildenberg, Fred CGJ Sweep, Johannes G van der Hoeven, Peter Pickkers. Voluntary Activation of the Sympathetic Nervous System and Attenuation of the Innate Immune Response in Humans." *PNAS* 111, no. 20 (May 20, 2014): 7379-84.
doi: 10.1073/pnas.1322174111

[70] Matthias Wittfoth, "Hormetic Hypoxia," *The Wim Hof Method Blog*, October 31, 2019. https://www.wimhofmethod.com/blog/hormetic-hypoxia

[71] Marwa Azab, Ph.D. The Brain on Fire: Depression and Inflammation: Studies Show that There is a Link Between Inflammation and Depression," *Psychology Today*, October 29, 2018. https://www.psychologytoday.com/us/blog/neuroscience-in-everyday-life/201810/the-brain-fire-depression-and-inflammation.

[72] Francis E Lotrich, Mordechai Rabinovitz, Patricia Gironda, Bruce G Pollock. Depression Following Pegylated Interferon-alpha:Characteristics and Vulnerability. *Journal of Psychosomatic Research* 63, no. 2 (2007): 131 135.

https://doi.org/10.1016/j.jpsychores.2007.05.013

[73] Wayne State University - Office of the Vice President for Research. "Brain mechanisms that give The Iceman unusual resistance to cold: The findings suggest that his method could be relevant for management of some autoimmune and psychiatric disorders." *ScienceDaily*. February 28, 2018. www.sciencedaily.com/releases/2018/02/180228164934.htm (accessed September 30, 2019).

[74] Muzik, Reilly, Diwadkar. Brain over Body.

[75] Otto Muzik, Kaise T Reilly, Vaibhav A Diwadkar, Brain Over Body: A Study on the Willful Regulation of Autonomic Function during Cold Exposure, *NeuroImage* 172 (May 15, 2018): 632-41. doi: 10.1016/j.neuroimage.2018.01.067

[76] Edward Fitzpatrick Crangle. *The Origin and Development of Early Indian Contemplative Practices, Studies in Oriental Religions* 29 (Wiesbaden: Harrassowitz Verlag, 1994).

[77] Deepak Sarma. *Classical Indian Philosophy: A Reader* (New York: Columbia University Press, 2011), 196 - 97.

[78] PR Bhuyan. *Swami Vivekananda: Messiah of Resurgent India* (New Delhi: Atlantic Publishers & Distributors, 2003).

[79] The Immigration Act of 1924 (The Johnson-Reed Act), *U.S Department of State: Office of the Historian*, https://history.state.gov/milestones/1921-36/immigration-act (accessed February 26, 2020)

[80] Richard Rosen. Walt Baptiste, *Yoga Journal*, April 5, 2017. https://www.yogajournal.com/yoga-101/walt-baptiste

[81] Michelle Goldberg. Iyengar and the Invention of Yoga, *The New Yorker*, August 23, 2014. https://www.newyorker.com/business/currency/iyengar-invention-yoga

[82] Andrew Harvey, Karuna Erickson. *Heart Yoga: The Sacred Marriage of Yoga and Mysticism* (Berkeley: North Atlantic Books, 2010).

[83] Swami Veda Bharati. *Yogi in the Lab: Future Directions of Scientific Research in Meditation* (Reishikesh, India: Himalayan Yoga Publications Trust, 2006).

[84] Andreas Michalsen, Paul Grossman, Ayhan Acil, Jost Langhorst, Rainer Lüdtke, Tobias Esch, George Stefano, Gustav Dobos. Rapid Stress Reduction and Anxiolysis Among Distressed Women as a Consequence of a Three-Month Intensive Yoga Program, *Medical Science Monitor: International Medical Journal of Experimental and Clinical Research* 11, no. 12, (December 2005).
https://www.ncbi.nlm.nih.gov/pubmed/16319785/?report=abstract

[85] Caroline Smith, Heather Hancock, Jane Blake-Mortimer, Kerena Eckert. A Randomised Comparative Trial of Yoga and Relaxation to Reduce Stress and Anxiety, *Complementary Therapies in Medicine* 15, no. 2 (June 2007). doi: 10.1016/j.ctim.2006.05.001

[86] M Javnbakht, R Hejazi Kenari, M Ghasemi. Effects of Yoga on Depression and Anxiety of Women, *Complementary Therapies in Clinical Practice* 15, no. 2 (May 2009).
doi: 10.1016/j.ctcp.2009.01.003

[87] Bessel A van der Kolk, Laura Stone, Jennifer West, Alison Rhodes, David Emerson, Michael Suvak, Joseph Spinazzola. Yoga as an Adjunctive Treatment for Posttraumatic Stress Disorder: a Randomized Controlled Trial, *The Journal of Clinical Psychiatry* 75, no. 6 (June 2014): 559-65. doi: 10.4088/JCP.13m08561

[88] A Vedamurthachar, Nimmagadda Janakiramaiah, Jayaram M Hegde, Taranath K Shetty, DK Subbakrishna, SV Sureshbabu, BN Gangadhar. Antidepressant Efficacy and Hormonal Effects of Sudarshana Kriya Yoga (SKY) in Alcohol Dependent Individuals, *Journal of Affective Disorders* 94, no. 1-3 (August 2006): 249-53. doi: 10.1016/j.jad.2006.04.025

[89] Julienne E Bower, Gale Greendale, Alexandra D Crosswell, Deborah Garet, Beth Sternlieb, Patricia A. Ganz, Micheal R Irwin, Richard Olmstead, Jesusa Arevalo, Steve W Cole. Yoga Reduces Inflammatory Signaling in Fatigued Breast Cancer Survivors: a Randomized Controlled Trial, *Psychoneuroendocrinology* 43 (May 2014): 20-9. doi: 10.1016/j.psyneuen.2014.01.019

[90] Veeran Subramaniam, Gregory YH Lip. Hypertension to Heart Failure: a Pathophysiological Spectrum Relating Blood Pressure, Drug Treatments and Stroke, *Expert Review of Cardiovascular Therapy* 7, no. 6 (June, 2009). doi: 10.1586/erc.09.43

[91] J Yogendra, HJ Yogendra, S Ambardekar, RD Lele, S Shetty, M

Dave, N Husein.. Beneficial Effects of Yoga Lifestyle on Reversibility of Ischaemic Heart Disease: Caring Heart Project of International Board of Yoga, *The Journal of the Association of Physicians of India* 52 (April 2004): 283-9. https://www.ncbi.nlm.nih.gov/pubmed/15636328

[92] Lorenzo Cohen, Carla Warneke, Rachel T Fouladi, M Alma Rodriguez, Alejandro Chaoul-Reich. Psychological Adjustment and Sleep Quality in a Randomized Trial of the Effects of a Tibetan Yoga Intervention in Patients with Lymphoma, *Cancer* 100, no. 10 (May 15, 2004): 2253-260. doi: 10.1002/cncr.20236

[93] PJ John, Neha Sharma, Chandra M Sharma, Arvind Kankane. Effectiveness of Yoga Therapy in the Treatment of Migraine without Aura: a Randomized Controlled Trial, *Headache: The Journal of Head and Face Pain* 47, no. 5 (May 2007): 654-61. doi: 10.1111/j.1526-4610.2007.00789.x

[94] Colombian FARC Peace Deal: The Man Behind the Peace Breakthrough, *Art of Living*, 2016. https://www.artofliving.org/de-en/colombian-farc-peace-deal-man-behind-peace-breakthrough

[95] Lawrence Becker. *A History of Western Ethics* (New York: Routledge, 2003), 27.

[96] Donald Robertson. *Stoicism and the Art of Happiness: Practical Wisdom for Everyday Life* (New York: The McGraw Hill Companies, 2013).

[97] Lawrence C Becker, *A New Stoicism* (Princeton: Princeton University Press, 2001).

[98] Keith Seddon. *Epictetus' Handbook and the Tablet of Cebes: Guides to Stoic Living* (New York: Routledge, 2005): 217.

[99] Epictetus, *Discourses*.

[100] Lucius Annaeus Seneca. *Letters from a Stoic: All Three Volumes*, translated by Richard Mott Gummere (Enhanced Media, 2016): 97.

[101] Ryan Holiday. What Building a Country Requires, *The Daily Stoic*, July 4, 2018. https://dailystoic.com/what-building-a-country-requires

[102] Ryan Holiday. The Definitive List of Stoicism in History & Pop Culture, *The Daily Stoic*. https://dailystoic.com/stoicism-pop-culture

[103] James Bond Stockdale. *Courage Under Fire: Testing Epictetus's Doctrines*

in a Laboratory of Human Behavior (Stanford: Board of Trustees of the Leland Stanford Junior University: Hoover Essays no. 6, 1993).

[104] Tim Ferriss. Why You Should Define Your Fears Instead of Your Goals | Tim Ferriss," *Ted Talks, YouTube*, July 14, 2017. https://www.youtube.com/watch?v=5J6jAC6XxAI

[105] Seneca, Moral letters to Lucilius: On Anger.

[106] Seneca. Moral Letters to Lucilius: *Letters from a Stoic*, 83.2.

[107] Peter Fenwick. What Really Happens When You Die | End of Life Phenomena, *Thanatos TV: At Home with Peter Fenwick, YouTube*, May 2, 2018. https://www.youtube.com/watch?v=78SkTuk8Zd4

[108] Alan Watts. "Out of Your Mind 02: The Nature of Consciousness," recorded 1969, streaming audio, accessed May 30, 2022. https://www.organism.earth/library/document/out-of-your-mind-2.

[109] Adam Hadhazy. Think Twice: How the Gut's 'Second Brain' Influences Mood and Well-Being, *Scientific American*, February 12, 2010. https://www.scientificamerican.com/article/gut-second-brain

[110] M Nathaniel Mead. Benefits of Sunlight: A Bright Spot for Human Health. *Environmental Health Perspectives* 116, no. 4 (April 2008): 160-67. doi: 10.1289/ehp.116-a160.

[111] James L. Oschman, Gaétan Chevalier, Richard Brown, "The effects of grounding (earthing) on inflammation, the immune response, wound healing, and prevention and treatment of chronic inflammatory and autoimmune diseases," *Journal of Inflammation Research* vol. 8 83-96. Mar.24, 2015), doi:10.2147/JIR.S69656. https://www.ncbi.nlm.nih.gov/pmc/articles/PMC4378297/

[112] Kris Gunnars. 10 Health Benefits of Low-Carb and Ketogenic Diets, *Healthline*, November 20, 2018. https://www.healthline.com/nutrition/10-benefits-of-low-carb-ketogenic-diets#section6

[113] Ellen Loanes. Navy SEALs are Looking into the Keto Diet to be even more Effective on Missions, *Business Insider*, June 14, 2019. https://www.businessinsider.com/navy-seals-keto-diet-to-be-even-more-effective-2019-6

[114] Matt Walker. Sleep is your Superpower, *Ted Talks* Vancouver B.C., YouTube, April, 2019.
https://www.youtube.com/watch?v=5MuIMqhT8DM&t=3s

[115] https://en.wikipedia.org/wiki/Attachment_theory

[116] Michael Woods. Mike Tyson Says 'Toad Venom' Has Changed His Life, *Ring TV*, January 18, 2019. https://www.ringtv.com/552565-mike-tyson-says-toad-venom-has-changed-his-life.

[117] Anonymous testimonials provided by Safe Spaces Amsterdam. https://www.safespacesamsterdam.com

[118] Wesley Thoricatha, "'I Think I Can Leave Afghanistan in the Past': Interview with a Military Psychologist about MDMA Therapy for PTSD," Psychedelic Times, April 16, 2019. https://psychedelictimes.com/i-think-i-can-leave-afghanistan-in-the-past-interview-with-a-military-psychologist-about-mdma-therapy/?fbclid=IwAR01PWuNsfwHN2IDnWIRrE8JYNx7OagcbuFZpw8GKnuTO4ul983l

[119] Doug Steiny. In 8 Months I was Completely Symptom-free | Wim Hof Method Experience," Wim Hof Method Experience, *YouTube*, August 23, 2019.
https://www.youtube.com/watch?v=1nOv4aNiWys&list=PLgpy0mvhxvqiFmb2hbKxdowXZQv2BWKyY&index=7&t=2s

[120] Brad Carson. Marine Corps Officer Experiences the Wim Hof Method," The Wim Hof Method, *YouTube*, September 13, 2019.
https://www.youtube.com/watch?v=I2znpVLk7pk&list=PLgpy0mvhxvqiFmb2hbKxdowXZQv2BWKyY&index=8&t=26s

[121] Anuschka Franken, Multiple Sclerosis | Wim Hof Method Testimonial, The Wim Hof Method, *YouTube*, January 4, 2016.
https://www.wimhofmethod.com/testimonials

[122] Darin Olien. Proper Nutrition And The Wim Hof Method For Optimal Health, The Wim Hof Method, *YouTube*, April 21, 2016.
https://www.wimhofmethod.com/testimonials

[123] Henk Van Den Bergh. Rheumatoid Arthritis Wim Hof Method Testimonial, The Wim Hof Method, *YouTube*, January 7, 2016.
https://www.wimhofmethod.com/testimonials

[124] Alistair Overeem. Alistair Overeem Talks Wim Hof Method, The Wim Hof Method, *YouTube*, March 3, 2016.

https://www.wimhofmethod.com/testimonials

[125] Laird Hamilton. Laird Hamilton Talks About the Wim Hof Method, The Wim Hof Method, *YouTube*, January 4, 2016.
https://www.wimhofmethod.com/testimonials

Made in United States
Troutdale, OR
08/08/2024